Books by Selden Rodman

Verse

THE AMAZING YEAR

THE REVOLUTIONISTS

THE AIRMEN

LAWRENCE: THE LAST CRUSADE

MORTAL TRIUMPH AND OTHER POEMS

Art

THE EYE OF MAN

PORTRAIT OF THE ARTIST AS AN AMERICAN

RENAISSANCE IN HAITI

HORACE PIPPIN: A NEGRO PAINTER IN AMERICA

Anthologies

ONE HUNDRED MODERN POEMS

ONE HUNDRED AMERICAN POEMS

WAR AND THE POET (WITH RICHARD EBERHART)

THE POETRY OF FLIGHT

A NEW ANTHOLOGY OF MODERN POETRY

Travel

HAITI: THE BLACK REPUBLIC

THE EYE OF MAN

Form and Content in Western Painting

Gruenewald

CRUCIFIXION

Dali

THE EYE OF MAN

Form and Content in Western Painting

by **SELDEN RODMAN**

As modern art forges ahead, it seems to become more and more indifferent to what art signified, whether deliberately or not, during untold ages: a form of man's awareness of the world. The sculptors of the Acropolis and the cathedrals, the painter of the Villeneuve Pietà, Michelangelo, Titian and Rembrandt really "possessed" a world; is not our art, born of a cleavage of man's consciousness, tending to "possess" no more than its private kingdom—that of painting?

— MALRAUX

The abstract is not life and everywhere draws out its contradictions. You can refute Hegel but not the Saint or the Song of Sixpence.

— YEATS

DEVIN-ADAIR · NEW YORK · 1955

To the memory of
my great-aunt Fannie Van Nostrand Ramsdell (1860–1940)
who first showed me vistas of this world
more splendid than Nature's
and to my daughter Oriana (1951–   )
who will inherit it.

CONTENTS

PART ONE

Prologue:

The Eye of God

Obin's Nativity. Its 'images'—everyday life in Cap Haitiën, 1954. Its 'form'—"the appropriate shapes an artist discovers in the process of saying what he has to say." Its 'influences'—none, though resemblances to Giotto, Rousseau and Orozco may be found. (*Hans Lownds collection.*)

PART ONE

Prologue:

The Eye of God

The purpose of this book is to examine a variety of efforts to interpret man's experience, and by so doing to throw light on the central question facing the artist in our time. That question broadly is: Has the artist any obligation to weigh human values or to communicate through his art a vision of spiritual truth? And conversely, does failure to acknowledge such responsibilities deny to the artist both the driving force on which the great arts of the past have soared and the audience without which the artist would seem to be doomed to commune with himself exclusively?

Even to state the question today is to take sides. For to suggest that the great artists of the past may have regarded their art as a vehicle for the transmission of "ideas"—whether in justifying God's ways to Man or in contributing to an understanding of the human situation—is to cast doubt upon the value of the major preoccupation of most serious artists in the last half-century: the preoccupation with form.

What is form? Is it, as many of the most gifted artists of this epoch believe, an end in itself? Or is it merely the appropriate shape an artist discovers in the process of saying what he has to say? In the complete work of art, form and content are indistinguishable; one is not immediately conscious of either. But in the formalistic, one is conscious of form, just as in the didactic one is apt to be disturbed by its inconsequence. Certainly without formal imagination, technical originality and an innate sense of how to arrange sounds, shapes or colors, there is no art at all. And just as certainly it is true that the post-Renaissance insistence upon stating the "content" of a work in terms of its illusionistic "reality" alone led to a neglect of formal values which could only be cured by a re-emphasis on the "abstract" relationships inherent in any art of real quality. But does it not just as basically follow that without serious *content*—a projection through tangible symbols of the artist's attachment to values outside art itself—all the formal virtues in the world add up to no more than decorative play? To say so is to commit, in the eyes of those dedicated to a "non-objective" art, a cardinal heresy.

3

Art as Personal Experience

As one who is neither a painter nor a professional critic, but rather a poet, a sometime co-worker with primitive muralists, and a life-long enthusiast of all the arts, it seems appropriate that I should preface the attempted resolution of this heresy with an account of the personal experiences that led me to commit it. In a scholarly work this would be neither necessary nor appropriate. But there is a question whether values can be defined or re-defined by scholarship. In any event this book, though written with respect for scholarship and taking the knowledge and analysis of art experts into consideration wherever possible, is written by a layman and addressed to other laymen.

Works of art cannot be evaluated, analyzed or related one to another unless they are first felt. And feeling a work of art—experiencing the initial shock to one's nervous system, being blinded by the artist's vision, and living in the subsequent splendor of that revelation with at least a momentary conviction that the world can never be the same—is a wholly personal experience.

Perhaps it has been the belated recognition of this fact, historically speaking, that has led to our difficulty. So anxious has the critic been to identify himself with the God-given intuition of the artist that he has been willing to forswear his historic role as a middleman in the chain of communication. In his new-found love affair with the producer he has turned his back completely on the consumer. Wouldn't concern for such long-abused considerations as "God" and "love" arouse the suspicion that he was lacking in spirit and heart? He may even have felt that the artist, whose approach to these matters in the act of creation *must* be intuitive (hadn't he, the critic, pointed this out?) would resume calling him a philistine.

To protect himself, then, the critic made a god of Form.

Art Has Two Faces

The result of this deification of form has been that art, whose particular glory consisted in its having two faces (it was the justifiable business of the artist to strive to make them indistinguishable), for the time being sacrificed one.

Now while the element of *content* in works of art has never, until today, suffered a total eclipse, its subordination in times of retreat from life or cynicism has been a recurrent phenomenon. In such times artists have been detached from the community or have deliberately withdrawn from it to concern themselves with formal problems, leaving to a few eccentrics or isolated rebels the strain of reinventing a common expressive language. In times of generally accepted social values, on the other hand, even the less gifted and courageous have managed to create aesthetically satisfying forms out of the commonly accepted myths and images.

This is a good place to define terms. Formalism with a capital F will be used to designate that particular movement (rising to self-consciousness in the art of Manet and Cézanne) which reached its logical climax in the non-objective abstraction of today; formalism, uncapitalized, will describe any period or tendency in art that has exhibited preoccupation with form at the expense of other values. Those other values, having to do with an artist's human or spiritual commitments, with his projection of relationships in the world outside art itself, will be designated *expressive content*. The term content alone, since it is generally regarded as synonymous with representational subject matter or even mere illustrative storytelling, does not serve to define the antithesis of the formalistic. The aim of the Second Part of this book will be to seek out those moments in the history of Western painting when the artist's preoccupations with expressive content and form were in healthy equilibrium.

Philomé Obin's Eye of God (detail from "Crucifixion" in Cathedral St.-Trinité, Port-au-Prince, Haiti, showing adjacent mural by Rigaud Benoit, left). Journeyman work—designing rosters for a local Masonic temple—provided the primitive artist with an appropriate symbol.

The Eye of God

During the winters of 1950 and 1951, while directing the mural work of the primitive painters in the apse and transepts of Haiti's Cathedral St.-Trinité [1], I received clear confirmation of two long-cherished beliefs.

The first was that if artists should once more engage their expressive capacity to give effective form to a theme of meaningful human content, they would inevitably re-open the door to communication. The fact that

---

[1] I have described this accomplishment in *Haiti: The Black Republic*, New York, Devin-Adair, 1954, pp. 94-105; the earlier development of the artists who participated in the mural work was related in *Renaissance in Haiti*, New York, Pellegrini & Cudahy, 1948.

Sketch for the scene below the Eye. Obin's involvement in his community—in this case, observation of neighbors' refusal to commit themselves to the storms of passing revolutions—provided the expressive content for a popular religious masterpiece.

the content of these murals was "spiritual" as well as "human" increased their communicative potential for a society that still participated actively in religious ceremonies from early childhood till death; but it served to remind one also that whereas religion had inspired most of the world's humanly meaningful arts, *spiritual content* in the past few centuries of our religiously institutionalized and sceptical era had become more and more the preserve of the unorthodox individual seeker after truth and less and less of the professional maker of devotional images. Here in Haiti, where no such paradox existed, where people had no art except what they might make for themselves, where an artist was a man of the people and every peasant to some degree still an artist, there was little likelihood that the religious symbol would be perfunctory. As a matter of fact, the most sophisticated modern painter and the lowliest charcoal burner were equally moved by the murals—and the latter had no more difficulty "reading" them than the former. The artist responded because the forms and colors were fresh, the symbols and images felt. The peasant accepted the formal innovations because his taste was still relatively unaffected by the debased canons of Western illustration; but it was the *content*, as expressed through these fresh forms, that moved him.

My second belief had been that the creative process, even if defined in terms of the magic of formal invention alone, comes to birth most easily *as a by-product of extended cultivation in a field concerned with some one or all of life's non-formal values.* Other factors being equal, the less self-consciously an artist sets about producing "art," the more likely he is to come up with it. To quote Wilfred Owen's famous dictum: "Above all I am not concerned with Poetry. My subject is War and the pity of War. The Poetry is in the pity. . . ." Who will deny that the richest poetry the world knows is imbedded in the plays of Shakespeare, Sophocles and Racine, the epics of Dante, Vergil and Milton?

The Eye of God, in Obin's St.-Trinité mural, looks out from a cloud upon the Crucifixion below. I painted that cloud, under the primitive artist's direction and at his suggestion, and as I did so I had time to reflect upon the meaning of the phenomenon below me. Under this all-seeing Eye the Christian pageant was unfolding once more, not distantly like a hieratic dance of untouchable preceptors, but here and now: Christ, the suffering and betrayed but undefeated Hero of Humanity; the Virgin, wonderstruck amid the blindly unconcerned of marketplace and laundry; the Marriage at Cana, a country wedding; and all the participators, Galilean or Haitian, who saw nothing unusual happening: ourselves.

A Modern with Content

Obviously there were limits to what could be deduced from an experiment, no matter how successful, with self-taught artists in an environment isolated for centuries from the main currents of Western art.

The only contemporary American artist who seemed at that time to be employing the resources of painting in a fresh way to present a commentary on life as broad as the Haitians' was Ben Shahn. And curiously, Shahn's style, deliberately employing a form of poetic caricature sharpened with the primitive, resembled Obin's. Our joint recognition of this affinity, at an exhibition of Obin's work I had brought to New York, led to a biography of the American artist [2] and an exploration of the relation of form and content in modern art as seen through the eyes of one of its most distinguished exponents.

Shahn, confronted by the abstractions of the Non-objective [3] school, had asserted that he guessed the trouble was he didn't care that much about art; he was interested primarily in life, and in art only in so far as it enabled him to express what he felt about life. Admitting that he himself had never been a religious man, he added that after seeing the Giottos, Masaccios, and Angelicos in a recent loan collection he had been forced to realize that religion had furnished "the warmest, the tenderest, the most beautiful content that art has had so far." Form was merely the shape taken by content. Art was the celebration of the actual. "There's a difference," he had continued, "in the way a $25 coat wrinkles from the way a $75 coat wrinkles. It's just as important aesthetically as the difference in light of the Ile de France and the Brittany Coast. Maybe it's more important."

This was only Shahn's way of saying that the time had come for the artist to emerge from his studio and mingle with other men again, all kinds of men, if he wanted to paint pictures that would communicate on either a human or a supra-human level. The time, he seemed to be saying, was later than any of us thought; unless the artist identified himself with those concerned for the salvation of threatened personality, he might not only find himself among the faceless: he might wake up in no world at all.

But Shahn, for all his adaptability, was becoming almost as isolated a figure in his way as Obin. As late as 1939, or even 1943, his way of painting promised to become the dominant mode, but with the end of the War and the disillusionment with political radicalism that followed it, social criticism in any degree fell out of favor. Shahn himself, denied the walls as well as the audience his genius demanded, began to mine a vein of oblique fantasy that had hitherto played a secondary role in his pictures.

Extending the Search: Los Angeles

Setting out for California in the winter of 1952 I had determined to talk with a different kind of artist, one who was closer to the mainstream of European painting and who, no matter how much he might have to say, shared that preoccupation with form which seemed to obsess most of the serious artists of our century. Shahn had been perhaps too healthy an artist to be typical of this age of anxiety. Nor did art seem to be moving

■

[2] *Portrait of the Artist as an American* by Selden Rodman, New York, Harper, 1951.
[3] This broad term will be used throughout the book to include all post-Cubist abstractionists—"geometrical" as well as "biomorphic" or "abstract expressionist"; distinctions between them are discussed on page 129.

Ben Shahn's "Cherubs and Children." Painted during World War II, this was the first of the artist's pictures to employ dream fantasy in the manner of the surrealists—but to a compelling human and social purpose.

in the direction of Shahn's anecdotal pictures of the late Thirties and early Forties; Shahn himself, in fact, seemed to be moving away from them. Rico Lebrun, who lived in Los Angeles and who had just finished a series of impressive semi-abstract paintings and drawings dealing with the Crucifixion, might throw new light on the contemporary artist's dilemma, partly out of the experience of his own unresolved struggle and partly from his extraordinary knowledge of the problems of the Old Masters.

Before I had settled down to exploring these questions with Lebrun, however, two unexpected visual experiences and a chain of events involving the local community's attitude toward the arts served to re-focus my attention on the ever-widening abyss between the modern artist and the public.

The impact of the city itself did so. Lebrun then lived in a model

Aimee Semple McPherson. Press photograph showing the famous evangelist in a typical pose. Resulting illustrative image reflects a community's desire to settle for religion's historical (formalistic) values rather than its living (expressive) ones.

housing development in a section of Los Angeles surrounded by oil derricks, television masts, supermarkets and the abandoned sets for "Gone with the Wind." The miles and miles of lonely streets and houses, the parks and cafeterias, the drive-in theatres and drive-in restaurants I had to pass every day to get there, reminded me that this was a place adorned with imports—a village increased by all the villages of Iowa, Nebraska, Oklahoma and Missouri that had proliferated over hundreds of square miles without ever achieving definition. The people themselves were not the only imports. The trees, the shrubs, the flowers, even the water and the soil had been brought in from elsewhere to disguise a desert. I thought of Los Angeles' pervasive fear that the artificial water resources will give out some day, and of the even more pervasive fear that human resources will dry up. I thought of Nathaniel West's description of the migrants who discovered that sunshine isn't enough. "They get tired of oranges, even of avocadoes and passion fruit," he had written. "Nothing happens. They don't know what to do with their time. They haven't the mental equipment for leisure, the money nor the physical equipment for pleasure." Was

Oscar de Mejo's "Christ in Hollywood." A sophisticated neo-primitive seizes upon the satirical implications of contemporary lip-service to religious truth.

this atmospheric sickness ascribable to the character of the people as exiles, I wondered, to their detachment and uprootedness in an alien clime, or rather to the trivial and ephemeral nature of most occupations? There were more schools to teach trades and more service occupations here than in any city in the United States, yet in only somewhat less acute forms, I realized, both aspects of alienation applied to the whole country. Still, the symbolism forced itself upon one most insistently here. Manufacturing caskets for animals, running a dog's beauty parlor or renting moths and butterflies to the movie companies are not occupations that give one a sense of either earthly or eternal values. I thought of the "new paganism" in Los Angeles' famous cults, from Krishnamurti and Aimee Semple Mc-Pherson to The Mighty I Am Presence and Mankind United. I thought of a friend who had just moved East in disgust after painting a picture of the Second Coming—Christ besieged by reporters and autograph hunters. But I found the desire to exorcize the tragic and the eternal by escaping into the present focused most dramatically in a cemetery.

Art of the Academy: Forest Lawn

It was when confronted with the celebration of humane and spiritual values revealed in such pseudo-classical sculptures as "Faithful Friends," "Mother Love," "Unfaltering Trust," "Spiritual Grace," "Tranquil Memories," "Dreams of Peace" and the like, that I began to understand why so many modern artists set their teeth against human and spiritual values. It isn't the values that repel them but the tired and shopworn imagery dear to the public. The *living* arts of today, like all those coming to fruition in times of unrest and doubt, are basically concerned with death. Was it

"Art for the People, I. Detail of Ernesto Gazzeri's monumental work at Forest Lawn Memorial Park. This is one of the most thought-stirring sculptural groups ever created and is the subject of many sermons. Dr. Hubert Eaton, Forest Lawn's founder, has said, 'The sculptor and I discussed many interpretations, but the one I like best is found in the words of Victor Herbert's immortal song, "Ah, Sweet Mystery of Life." ' " (Caption by Forest Lawn.)

surprising that the art chosen to represent Forest Lawn's (and Los Angeles') preoccupation with "staying alive" was an art that had been dead for more than twenty centuries?

The genesis of this symbolism dated back to 1916 when Dr. Hubert Eaton became Forest Lawn's director (he prefers the word Builder) and decided to build a cemetery that would be "heartening and restful," where there would be "no bleak symbols of mourning" and where although "beauty costs money" one could have "an investment which constantly is increasing in value and which none of life's adversities can take from you." Believing that "beauty helps to strip from death its fearsome associations," the Builder had determined to gather together in Forest Lawn "objects of art, architecture, history and romance—those that educate and uplift a community."

The two most impressive of these art objects that confronted me were the eighteen life-size allegorical figures called "The Mystery of Life" and the "Crucifixion" painting by Jan Styka. Professor Ernesto Gazzeri carved his symbolic fountain group, we are told, "because Forest Lawn has solved the mystery of life." The individual figures are best described in the official literature. Among them are "a boy who is astonished at the miracle that has happened in his hand—one moment an unbroken egg; the next a chick, teeming with life. 'Why?' he asks, 'How does it happen? What is the answer to this mystery of life?'" His Grandmother—is too resigned to answer him. The Sweet Girl Graduate—is lost in dreams. The Lovers "who believe they have found the answer in love's first kiss" ignore the Scientist, who is "troubled," the philosopher "who scratches his puzzled head in vain" and the Atheist, "the fool, who grinningly cares not at all." The happy family group is "not too perturbed by the mystery although even they seem to ask 'Why do the doves mate?'"[4]

It would be impossible to add much to such explicit directions. Their banality is in every way realized by the artist. Every implication of the word "mystery" is denied. The function of art is reduced to the reproduction of types from vaudeville or the class yearbook. Formal values have yielded to content completely. There is no communication of experience— nor any inkling that the artist has had any experience to communicate. Death, surely the supreme mystery of life, before which even Christ in his great faith weakened and cried out in protest, is brushed aside in a calendar quatrain:

> *There is nothing to trouble any heart,*
> *Nothing to hurt at all:*
> *Death is only a quiet door*
> *In an old wall.*

Less startling in its denial of the fear of death but even more astonishing in its repudiation of the resources of art, is Jan Styka's "Crucifixion," the world's largest oil painting, which hangs in a tomb of its own. It is 195 feet long and 45 feet high. Its creator was a Polish artist who died in 1925. Every hour on the hour the huge canvas is enveiled by the drawing of a curtain weighing 3500 pounds before a hushed audience which sits in theatre seats "upholstered in rich burgundy" listening to soft music— and a Voice. The Voice, with an assist from a projected arrow of light which jumps from head to head, quotes Scripture to inform us where each participant was and what he was doing at this supreme moment of history.

"At this dark hour . . ." the Voice intones while the landscape unfolds. Save for Christ's lost figure between two crosses on the central pla-

■

[4] *Art Guide of Forest Lawn.* Glendale, California. No date.

"Art for the People, II. More people visit Forest Lawn in an average year than visit New York's Metropolitan Museum. Here is shown the central section of Jan Styka's dynamic painting, 'The Crucifixion,' noted for its fidelity to Biblical history—and one of the reasons for the Memorial Park's popularity and world fame." (Caption by Forest Lawn.)

teau, there is nothing to indicate that this is not a tinted photo-mural of some "location" in the Mojave Desert for the next de Mille extravaganza. The antlike crowds of "extras," the picturesque peasants posing against ruins, the retired businessmen and their wives sunbathing on the roofs of their palaces, the monolithic walls that seem to be painted on movable screens, the angry sky with just enough sunlight breaking through in shafts to promise a better day—all have the master's touch. Even the central scene is there to remind us that the creator of the "Greatest Show on Earth" recreated the Passion a generation before Darryl Zanuck conceived it in Cinemascope. To be sure, this scene could have been filmed somewhere in the Middle East, perhaps near one of the Crusaders' castles; and we are not surprised to learn that Styka, considering it essential to "authenticate" his conception, made a pilgrimage to Palestine to sketch the reputed location before setting brush to canvas.

What is there in this deification of optical realism that makes such a picture at once incapable of conveying spiritual truth and aesthetically acceptable to the largest educated public in history? Religion—at least the Christian religion as revealed in the Scriptures—is here regarded as *his-*

Crucifixion set from Darryl Zanuck's cinemascope "Jerusalem," illustrating similarity of intent between academic painting, as exemplified in the Styka "Crucifixion," and American moving-picture making for the middle classes. Outward spectacle, not inner truth, is depicted in both cases.

tory: something remote and static and picturesque, something to be endured passively Sundays as a de Mille picture is to be endured Saturday night or a Tournament of Roses on New Year's Day. We are not transported, as Michelangelo transports us, to a supra-human world of divinely proportioned heroes, enclosing human frailty and fallibility in the mystery of a perfect harmony. Nor is the myth brought home to us personally as in Gruenewald or Rembrandt, by the terrible juxtaposition of naked human suffering and divine compassion. The American middle class still conceives of art as having no relation to life: its function is the reproducing of scenes from literature; its component figures (Greco-Roman) are those accepted in the textbooks as "beautiful." These figures are only slightly modified by the ideal of the Hollywood movie-star, a face untroubled by thought which smiles blandly at the citizen in a thousand disguises from birth to death. A face of great beauty, telling its story in lines as expressive as the contours of the earth, is treated by one of the face-lifting specialists of Sunset Strip to resemble all other faces, and thus, by the removal of its personality, to conform to the middle class aesthetic norm.

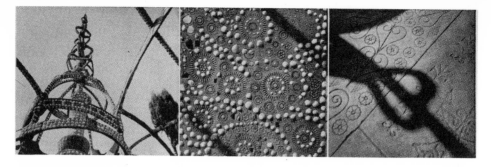

Details from Radilla's towers. Although intent is communicative, result is abstraction, because artist-artisan (unlike his counterpart in earlier times) is out of human contact with his audience.

The Artist Nobody Knows

I found the antithesis of this art, quite by accident, in the same city.

Watts, the Negro district of Los Angeles, lies in a no-man's-land of deteriorating bungalows that stretches interminably through the featureless flats between Pasadena, the upper-middle-class Nirvana, and Long Beach, the end of the road from Iowa, which has been called a cemetery with lights.

Here, thirty-three years ago, and still living in an anonymity as pervasive as that surrounding any of its citizens, the most dedicated artist in America began to build one of the strangest and most abstractly beautiful structures in the world—out of junk.

The highest tower is over a hundred feet high and still growing. In fact Simon Radilla, attached by his window cleaner's belt to the webbing like a benevolent spider, was adding a new series of flying buttresses—7-Up bottles with their orange labels facing out—the day I visited him. This tower had been only 25 feet high in 1922. A fresh set of necklaces brought it up to thirty, and so on. After the metal rods and mesh and a mixture of waterproof cement, come the artifacts of our civilization: orange-squeezers, bottle-caps, hub-caps, willow ware, percolators, hair setters, telephone insulators, burnt-out bulbs, tooth mugs, pieces of old mirrors, a glass shoe, a three-fingered bowling ball. There is no conscious choice of objects just as there is no deliberate plan in their arrangement. (In this respect, at least, Simon is at one with the Non-objective painters.) The objects are whatever is discarded, available in quantity and resistant to time and tremor. The design is always mysteriously incomplete. Seventy-five thousand sea shells embedded in the stern of this triangular ironclad would be overpowering if arranged symmetrically. As they are, in half circles and broken spokes of low relief, the effect is something like the awesome confusion of stars in the Milky Way. Only slightly more conventional are the volutes and cake stamps stenciled into the pavement, the concave "fossils" of Simon's hammer, compass and chisel in the lunette of the side walls, the rhythmic corncobs and ears of wheat like emblems of fertility above the fountains. These, too, are removed from the commonplace by being always sprained a little off their centers. Most astonishing is the seemingly unerr-

Towers of Simon Radilla, Watts, California. Eccentric art of a rebellious outcast from society, constructed of the "content" of mechanized urban life: reinforced concrete, tools once devoted to craftsmanship, fragmented *objets d'art,* mass-produced containers.

ing taste with which fragmented tiles of a thousand varieties are related in color-key and flow of design around the basins and stalagmite-like lesser outcroppings.

The walls around the towers were not part of Simon's plan. For all the obscurity in which the towers have grown, his will to communicate, to make their beauty available to everyone (it is in these respects that he parts company with the Non-objectivists) is as strong today as it ever was. The local police saw a hazard to climbing children, so the walls were built.

Simon was born in Italy in 1898, emigrating to the United States nine years later. Discharged from the Army Engineers in 1918 after serving in France, he resolved to begin work on his contribution to peace at once.

Huntington Hartford displaying examples of "good" and "bad" art. The "bad," topped confusingly by great Catholic expressionist Rouault, included also Miró, Kandinsky, Picasso. The "good": Homer, Gauguin, Cézanne and Mrs. Hartford's portrait of her husband.

"Why so many people want to shed blood?" he asks. "You go to boxing match. It's when nose is broken and blood flow over boxer's eyes that people clap for joy. That's why, my dear friend, I not turn on this radio my niece give me." Simon prefers to play ancient Martinelli and Caruso records on the horn-phonograph that is the only piece of furniture besides the bed in his one-room shack behind the towers. Every cent he has made, over food and taxes, in the past thirty-two years has gone into his masterwork. In the early days he set tiles and bought junk. Nowadays he works off and on for the telephone company, crawling through their underground conduits to plug overhead leaks with handfuls of wet plaster; but today the junk dealers give him their broken bottles and tiles so that all his money goes for the steel rods and wire mesh that he thinks have made the towers earthquake- and bomb-proof. He expects them to be a beacon of hope when the materialistic parts of the city have met the fate they deserve . . .

Whether Cambodia or any other exotic culture entered into Radilla's calculations is as doubtful as that he ever heard of the word "abstraction." That he saw San Marco or Monreale or Pompeii or the basilicas of Ravenna as a child is possible but not likely. All theorizings he answers with the simplicity of the true artist. "I had in mind to do something big and I did it." Was there a religious inspiration? "I believe in God, dear friend," he said, "but Christ He not crucified to build the power of the wealthy Church. That why I take down many years ago Cross that was on the highest tower there. Why? Because priest come and rub hands; he think Cross justify *him*!"

The deep furrows in Simon's leathery skin contract and he scratches his sparse graying hair when asked to supply logical connections between some of his statements. This bewilderment, and the obvious relish with which he describes the torments of Bruno and St. Simeon and identifies himself with their martyrdom, raises the question of his sanity. The question would be answered in the negative by the average man, not so much on the basis of what Simon says but of what he has built. Its relevance depends upon one's opinion of the degree of sanity expressed by the architecture of the norm—from the clapboard shanties of Watts and the hygienic glass ranch houses of Tarzana to the stone-and-steel office totems of the business center.

Art as Subversion

In November of 1951 the Los Angeles City Council made a determined effort to cut off funds for the Municipal Art Commission which had been sponsoring annual exhibits and prizes at the Greek Theatre. The pretext was that most of the prizes recently, instead of going to works of "traditional" character, had been awarded by the jury to work that was in the Council's words "modernistic, sacrilegious and communistic." Among the jurors was Rico Lebrun.

About the same time Huntington Hartford, a young philanthropist who had been financing scholarships for creative work at a community in nearby Pacific Palisades, wrote and published a pamphlet entitled *Has God Been Insulted Here?* The burden of it was that the modern artist had betrayed art and lost popular favor by ignoring the "normal people of this world," denouncing the "moneyed powers" and depicting "ugliness." Where, Hartford asked, was today's Raphael?

The public hearings of the Council opened with some pretty sensational charges, including one that a prize-winning picture of sailboats boldly displayed the hammer-and-sickle. Gerald Campbell, a 28-year-old combat veteran who had painted another equally innocuous prizewinner, a Graves-like landscape of mountain pines threaded against the setting sun, was grilled for an hour. One of the Councilmen remarked that the trees in this picture were not sufficiently well-rooted in the earth. A second thought that the moon was not round enough. A third suggested that the color red behind the trees could be taken to encourage sabotage of our natural resources. To which a fourth Councilman quite seriously added that it was a well-known fact that modern abstract art was a vehicle for espionage, constituting a code which supplied the Russians with the precise location of U.S. fortifications—"including Boulder Dam." A stylized "Crucifixion" in bronze by Bernard Rosenthal was shown to the Mayor by one of the Councilmen. "You are a Christian man," the latter shouted, "and you can't defend this kind of thing!"

The Mayor did, however, because the Councilmen had gone too far. The note on which public support could easily have been rallied had been struck by the chairman for a Coordinating Committee for Traditional Art. "The entire show," he had written the Mayor, "is a collection of meaningless daubs and lines with nothing that is uplifting or spiritual, only an affront to the sensibilities of normal people." Injection of the obviously ridiculous political charges had only served to make artists of all persuasions unite. When the Council on January 15, 1952, was finally forced to reverse itself, the reversal was correctly interpreted as a victory for freedom of expression rather than for modernism.

Hartford's pamphlet, published just as the hearings began, opened with some barracks talk from James Jones' novel *From Here to Eternity* and asked why it was that writers like Shakespeare weren't out to shock their readers and drag the top dogs down to the level of the bottom dogs:

> Engrossed with evil and the destruction of life to the point of seeing nothing but evil, he [the modern artist] has wandered off to some streamlined inferno in which he has burned in effigy the normal people of this earth . . . Will the time come once again when man will walk away from a work of art with elation instead of despair, of communion with a higher being and a conception of reality larger than life rather than a feeling that life has been reduced to its lowest common denominator?

After indicting modern music and the ballet in similar terms, Hartford asked what had happened to the painter of the modern world:

> Where is the Raphael of the sixteenth century or the Rubens of the seventeenth; where, indeed, is the Cézanne or the Van Gogh of the nineteenth? The painter of the twentieth century, more than the worker in any other of the fine arts, has become the slave rather than the master of his environment . . . little more than the fashionable author of a peep show to amuse the sophisticated and shock the ignorant. If he is not designing jewelry or stocking ads for slick magazines, then he is doing posters for the left-wing party of his country; if he is not discovering an art in the swift movement of flashlights before a camera, then he is turning out great indecipherable murals on the rape of the working class, or, according to the title of a recent picture, laying out "costume designs for a paranoic ballet."

The trouble was, Hartford concluded, that the voice of the malcontent is loudest in the land; that the artist suppresses his jealousy, refuses to adjust himself to society, seeking to achieve a world in which the weak may survive at the expense of the strong:

The work of art was and should again be the open forum in which all sides of a subject are discussed, with the conclusions of the artist definitely placing the right in the position of right, the wrong in the position of wrong, with no chance for men in brown shirts or black to twist his meaning . . .

Had Hartford been content to arraign modern art for its often excessively egocentric premises, its deficiency in humanity and its obsession with purely formal values, he would have been on firm ground. Unfortunately he tripped into the same pitfall as the Councilmen, assuming that an art opposed to realism, without sentiment or at odds with society, is in league with totalitarianism. On the contrary, the arts permitted in totalitarian countries have been without exception realistic (to the point of vying with photography), sentimental, and in fawning accord with the political status quo.[5]

But Hartford stumbled into several additional traps as well. Asking artists to be philosophical optimists and educators of the public in the ways of righteousness was to make a major error in aesthetics. Hartford was asking that art define truth rather than express it—and then defining it himself in the narrowest terms. Was art ever, as Hartford asserted, "an expression of the people, by the people, for the people"? Only at that point where the first artist (communicator) said what he had to say for all his fellows on the walls of the community cave. Thereafter, as a specialist in the language of visual communication, the artist would address himself to the *highest order* of individuals. Sometimes this audience would be a whole people in tune with his ideals, and sometimes not; the result in both cases was "for" those prepared to receive it. The true artist, in other words, is never primarily a moralist, he is first a poet, seeking to project his personal observation or vision of the world in terms of formal relationships. To demand of art a specific "moral answer" is just as unreasonable as to insist, as some formalist critics do, that the artist have no morals at all, that he create in a philosophical, scientific and religious vacuum.

The Artist Replies

It was in Los Angeles at precisely this moment that Rico Lebrun was finishing his "Crucifixion" series, a monumental expressive essay on one

■

[5] See page 140. Hartford acknowledges this in a more recent essay entitled "The Public Be Damned?" printed May 16, 1955, as a full page ad in the nation's leading newspapers. While taking many justified swipes at Formalism and its partisans, he continues to arraign modern artists—both formalistic and expressive—as engaged in some kind of a conspiracy. Rouault is among these conspirators for painting an "ugly" Christ. This is the nub of Hartford's confusion. He quotes with approval Keats' "Beauty is truth . . ." but he fails to fathom the definition. Rouault's prostitutes (page 30) are "ugly" enough to place last in any beauty contest, but they are thunderously true to life and to the Christian spirit the artist is illuminating by thus presenting them—and therefore beautiful as art.

Lebrun at work in Adams Boulevard studio on panel of "Crucifixion" triptych. A metaphorical world: the claw of the rooster on the arm of the Cross cast a shadow on the moon.

of the great spiritual themes of tradition that no museum could find permanent space for and no church offered to buy or even house. Lebrun's reaction to these two assaults served both to establish the modern artist's relation to the community and to introduce the thinking of one seeking in his work to deal with expressive content without sacrificing post-Cubist formal values.

It was from a pulpit that Lebrun (who looks rather like Savonarola) rose to answer the Council's challenge. What made him particularly indignant was that the jurors had given their time gratis, and that he seemed to have found in their company that lost community, stretching back through time from the Neapolitan streets of his boyhood to the Renaissance guilds: a community that couldn't be bought. And now these illiterate Jeremiahs whose ideas of art were based on the comic books were looking for blueprints of Oak Ridge in the most retiring of still lifes! "One would think," he said bitterly, "by the manner in which the community asks for our credentials on moral matters, on religion, on politics, that the community must at least sustain us, be responsible for our minimal security. But we, the artists who are asked all these questions, have but one characteristic in common—*we can't make a living.* So you see we are expected to be sober, cheerful, communicable, well-dressed, well-behaved and responsible to the community which does so much for us." Possibly it was overlooked, he added, that neglect is one of the main factors in the modern artist's life. "I would like to ask the professional men in this audience," he concluded, "How would you like to do dish-washing, carpentry, baby-sitting and floor walking in order to be able to carry on your profession? It is possible, just possible, that you might become unmanageable neurotics. . . ."

On the subject of Huntington Hartford, Lebrun thought a question more relevant than the whereabouts of today's Raphael was: Where is the de' Medici of the twentieth century? Hartford, had he risen above his environment, could have been one. As for artists "denouncing the moneyed powers," Lebrun couldn't think of a single painter who was doing that, at least directly, and, most not even indirectly. "The subject is too ephemeral." The trouble was that Hartford expected gratitude, and social gratitude at that, and he expected artists to change their styles to show it. Did the Medicis—or the Guggenheims or the Rockefellers—ask for gratitude? Or as Hartford seemed to be demanding, "for the portrayal of the philosophy of all's well with this best of all possible worlds"?

Who are the "normal people of this world," Lebrun wanted to know. "Did Greco paint them?" Did Gruenewald or Bosch? Goya? Van Gogh? Was Michelangelo's "Last Judgment" an assemblage of normal people? "I don't seem to remember many." Hartford's basic fallacy, Lebrun thought, was in refusing to acknowledge a superior life in painting itself whether in depicting the blessed or the damned. Which of the two you depicted, depended on the times and your temperament.

Behind the Council's ignorant animus and Hartford's earnest confusion, however, there lay a residual truth that Lebrun's impassioned defense should not blind us to. There is no reason to suppose that the average Florentine of the Quattrocento was a more discriminating judge of art than the middle class citizen of Los Angeles. It has even been questioned whether Lorenzo the Magnificent's appreciation went much beyond a shrewd appraisal of well-publicized names; certainly his collection of coins and cameos meant more to him than the young Michelangelo's marbles. The fact is that the Renaissance artists were dealing in themes and symbols that were common property and that most of them had a healthy respect for the public's approval of their degree of involvement in these themes if not for its taste. While Ghiberti was executing the bronze doors of the Baptistry in Florence, Vasari tells us, he invited the public to come to his shop and criticize his work as it progressed. In Los Angeles, on the contrary, as everywhere else in the modern world, most serious artists had long since withdrawn from any effort to deal meaningfully with subjects in which the public could be emotionally concerned. Against this snobbism the Council was fighting back with the only weapon in its meagre arsenal —philistinism—and Hartford with his slightly more mature plea for a reaffirmation of moral values.

Groping but sincerely, the new middle class, with a leisure for culture never known among so many in times past, yearns for some expression of its deeper needs. How inadequately those needs were being answered by a traditional art imposed from above had been revealed at Forest Lawn. I had also witnessed the touching but marginal attempt of "primitives" to salvage, outside society and high culture, a sincerity of self-expression owing nothing to aesthetic tradition. It remained to be seen to what extent a professional artist with the whole orchestration of Western painting at his command could succeed in bridging the widening chasm between content and form, spirit and reality, poet and public.

The "Crucifixion" of Rico Lebrun

Lebrun painted the "Crucifixion" because its theme promised to express the spiritual tragedy of his age in the metaphorical terms of his personal experience of that tragedy. When an architect had asked him how he could *afford* to paint it without a patron he had answered: "How often do you design a building and then go out and build it just because you want to see that kind of building built?" "We'd lose our shirts if we did that," the architect had answered, and Lebrun had replied: "Well, you have your answer."

There had been no lack of other large-scale offers. In March of 1940, for instance, the Philbrook Art Center of Tulsa, Oklahoma, had invited Lebrun to compete for a real mural on a real wall, listing among fourteen approved subjects: General Custer "with his long yellow curls" pursuing Black Kettle's horsemen. Or, in lighter vein: "Pipe Dream—an Indian sits beside a white man both smoking pipes; in the rising smoke from the white man's pipe is dimly depicted a big farm house, a red barn, a windmill, etc. In the smoke of the Indian's pipe are shown wide prairies, some buffalo running with Indians on spotted ponies pursuing them and shooting them with bows and arrows. . . ."

"It should be a self-evident premise," wrote Lebrun in answer to this offer, "that in the hands of a capable, or, possibly, extraordinary artist any subject matter may be treated with dignity."

> Unfortunately [he continued], such subjects as proposed are heavily handicapped by *a*) the pre-fabricated notions of the laymen offering the job—they "know nothing about painting but are very sure what Indians and pioneers looked like"—and *b*) by the enormous number of precedents set by the Savage-Manship tradition of a certain kind of "heroic and monumental" dignity, which, reducing all plastic symbols to a Pontiac Chief de Luxe approved by George Bridgman, sterilizes the image to such a forbidding extent that even bankers are impressed. How much contempt some of the American-born performers have shown for their great-great-grandfathers by their persistent addiction to this Prix de Rome calligraphy is well known. We could leave these un-American crimes to the State Capitols and mind our own business if they had not set such a dreadful precedent. I hope there is an American somewhere who, gifted with plastic powers, will

truly redeem the image of a pioneer and the trappings of a cattle-pony. I am a sort of fifth-rate cow-puncher myself, and I think of the Western saddle as one of the most beautiful objects in the world. But these images will have to be felt and conceived by an American—native or adopted—living in the world of today. They cannot be done according to historical record. It is *we* who make the historical record to our image and likeness, just as Greco made heaven look Spanish contemporary to Greco. In such processes the easily identified disappears; the uniforms and landmarks become a matter of danger unless a Piero or Paolo Uccello are on the job. If they are, those transformations will take place which precisely and inevitably cause the finished work to be condemned, since they will be precisely and inevitably conceived in the style of a valid plastic current—continents away from stylization. Perhaps the geological past of Oklahoma is more important, and certainly more durable as a legend, than any Daniel Boone. Oklahoma's land was being shaped millions of years before Boone, and it could be that its very own looks, inside the earth as well as outside on the prairie, will furnish the subject for a vast, *concrete factual* abstraction of fire and stone. Think, dear sirs, of the difficult task of integrating a muzzle-loader into a chromatic-plastic expanse of 13 x 70 feet! It would be lost, and with it the painter and his relation to the world after the Second and before the Third world wars.

. . . Your first move should be to abolish the theme of masquerade and pageantry and to *consult artists for possible themes before ever announcing the competition.* Under those circumstances I would do the utmost in my power—short of actually competing—if I should be called upon to help in any way.

The concrete, factual abstraction of stone and fire was something that Lebrun could speak of with feeling, for he had painted it, and would continue to paint it, for a decade. The sense of burning vehicle and molten

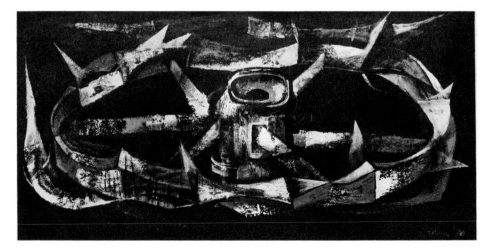

Lebrun's "Burning Spinner." St. Catherine's Wheel and the Crown of Thorns suggested by an image developed from drawings of a California brush fire.

flesh, of Anzio and Hiroshima, of man become metal and riven wood bleeding under the carpenter-executioner's axe, is in every picture of the Passion. As far back as 1939 when Lebrun dropped his facile draftsman's pencil for the pen "which can't be erased" and began to fill his sketchbooks with compulsive crosses and burning wheels, the subject was in the back of his mind. In the 40's when mechanized cavalry was crushing the bodies of free men, he had painted farm machinery in the field, twisted in brush fires,

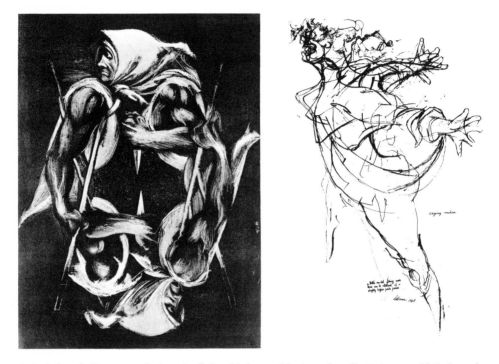

Left: Lebrun's "Beggar with Crutches" (trial lithograph). A profoundly Italian world, balanced precariously between comedy and tragedy; it persisted throughout the "Crucifixion" series, of whose sleeping soldiers Lebrun wrote: "They are animated combinations of turtle and man . . . reality treated metaphorically." *Right:* "Crying Machine" (drawing).

rained on, bleeding with rust. Later, when the horrors of Auschwitz and Buchenwald were being revealed, he had drawn butchers at their work, blasted tree-stumps and up-ended axles like tools of the torturer's trade. But the first conscious links in the chain were not forged until 1947 when the thought occurred to him that he could talk of something that *everybody* would be familiar with, a legend involving richness of pageantry, and at the same time a human story symbolizing the contemporary chronicle of man's inhumanity to man. To handle the most ordinary set of symbols with the most extraordinary means became his goal.

After youthful work in the classical tradition, Lebrun had gone through a phase which, much against his will, had allied him with the neo-Romantic movement. He had drawn beggars on crutches. The fact that people in rags and bandages blown into frantic farewells by precision bombing should appeal as "romantic" props was significant in itself, he thinks. "I imagine they recalled the *Thief of Bagdad* or the mob scenes of Hal Roach's studios to the citizens of the Bronx or Sunset Boulevard; but to me there was nothing romantic about this awful role of helplessness; contrariwise, something discouragingly ancient." With these Neapolitan figures he summed up, also, memories of participating in the theatricalism of street marionette shows. This fluctuating world, balancing precariously between comedy and tragedy, reality and make-believe, is profoundly Italian. It is manifested in the paintings of Caravaggio and Magnasco and it persists throughout the "Crucifixion" series, of whose sleeping soldiers Lebrun wrote: "They are animated combinations of turtle and man . . . reality treated metaphorically."

An art so ambitious and with so many antecedents could not fail to be tagged with the epithet "eclecticism," and indeed Lebrun's mature style, with its references to the masters of Mannerism and the Baroque on the one hand and to the Picasso of the "Guernica" on the other, infuriated the purists of every persuasion. Developing his theory of simultaneity in art partly as a result of experiences gained while teaching "animation" in the Disney studios, Lebrun had re-assessed his contemporaries, focusing on Picasso, Rouault, Orozco and Beckmann as the four great "animators" whose work was seen as silencing "the prattle about pure line" and "color for its own sake." They were the end of a tradition and those who asked to continue could not be expected to fill their shoes by the mere practise of "cosmic doodling." What Tintoretto had reached for in his "Massacre of the Innocents"—groups of figures spiraling in depth, rather than frontally presented as in the early Renaissance—had been fully realized in the "Guernica" (See page 122). For Picasso synthesized in effect the "wheel-spokes" of Tintoretto's lower-right-foreground group into a *single but multiple* image. The obligation in Tintoretto to keep each figure separate was discarded in our art, Lebrun thought, because the virtuosity of getting around the dilemma by tricks of perspective and chiaroscuro had become an end in itself. Tintoretto, being a Renaissance man, could not renounce the multiplication of figures, but he could *obscure that in the picture which he wished to de-emphasize*—in his case the anthropomorphic fixture of man in the pre-Copernican world. And he did this by means of chiaroscuro "which was not then just a technical way of illuminating an object" but a revolutionary insight into the nature of the world.

Does the "Crucifixion" series with its figures in tortured positions, hungry, emaciated, empty, starved for food and love, go back to the shock of the child's first loss, to the terror that comes from realizing that no matter how hard you may scream or kick, *you may die*? As Lebrun's symbols progressed from machine to woman to mother there was evident a recognition that the world's hunger and terror are a part of oneself. In the largest panel of the series the face of Christ was hidden, Lebrun said, because only so could it be taken for the face of any one of us. The ghoulish figure behind Christ represented the man "who just gets involved"—and so became culpable. "It could be taken as a warning to have nothing to do with that sort of action. Whenever we come to the point where no man in the nation or world can be persuaded to take such a job or fight other men, you can call this a civilized world. Because only He took that position, Christ, even in the Deposition, is alone."

It was not true, Lebrun asserted, that all these questions have nothing to do with painting. "You don't make a schoolmarm of yourself by being concerned with sentiment. The sentiments are what cause the altering and transformation of forms. The forms for the occasion then evolve. The transformation of the ladder in the 'Crucifixion' from a smooth one to an awful one, one hard to climb, is the transformation of the event graphically. The distance between one rung and the next is a psychological problem. The guy who climbed with the nails had to negotiate it. For Mondrian—I grant him that glory—the intervals are untroubled with psychological problems; they are beautifully solved problems of form and nothing more."

Lebrun dislikes comparisons but I manoeuvered him into making one more. He contrasted El Greco's simplicity with that of Georgia O'Keefe. "Greco marshals all the evidence in a complicated world before presenting his simplification." O'Keefe's simplicity was the simplicity "of a collar-bone or a horse-collar." The simplification of the so-called functional architects

Lebrun's "Soldier on Arm of Cross" (drawing). The artist obtained some of his expressive images by projecting photographs of sketches into a corner of the studio and then working from the resulting distortions.

was on the way out because the new modernists were beginning to realize that human beings need more than space and light. "They need design and curves and color and lots of other things too." Could you simplify love by cutting away all but its essence? "Our desire for simplicity, for 'triumphant solutions,' for accomplishment, for the clearcut and the wholly 'original' stems from our Puritanism. We have a fear of mud and blood. If we are to be anything," he concluded, "if we artists are to survive this period at all—which is by no means certain—we will survive as spokesmen, never again as entertainers."

Lebrun's "Crucifixion" triptych. Criticized for its superficial resemblance to Picasso's "Guernica" (see page 128), this huge monochrome was painted in six weeks preceding a show of the series, at the Los Angeles County Museum's request.

Summary and Forecast

What had I learnt? Substantially this:

1) The critic, realizing belatedly that art is a personal experience and must be felt before it can be evaluated, embraced the artist and turned his back on the audience for whom he had once served as intermediary.

2) Following this lead, or perhaps following his own inclination, the artist not only spurned society but began to create works in terms of the formal element of art alone—leaving *content* to the Academy and the primitives.

3) The art of the Academy, as I had seen it enshrined in the painting and sculpture of a famous cemetery, diverts (or "entertains") the public by

concealing its fear of death and simplifying its responses to life with a series of optimistic platitudes.

4) Even the art of primitives and eccentrics reflects more meaningfully the present time, being neither dishonest, imitative, "literary," uncommunicative nor egocentric.

5) As the gap widens between sophisticated artist and public, confusion is compounded by diversionary attacks. The artists, whether formalists or seekers after a new content, are accused by politicians of misleading the public, flouting tradition, contributing to subversion. Outraged moralists, sensing the unhealthy divorce between producer and consumer, accuse the modern artist of abdicating his role as a conveyor of truth, but make the aesthetic error of demanding that he *define* the good and the beautiful in his work rather than *express* it.

6) Most modernists retaliate with one or another version of Oscar Wilde's "There is no such thing as moral or immoral literature; there is only good writing and bad writing"—a confusion of the means with the end.

7) A few artists, "less concerned with art than with life," or recognizing that moral beliefs are among the non-aesthetic elements that "cause the transformation of forms," set their backs against the tide of fashion and seek to introduce expressive content into art without sacrificing form.

Since by this time the formalists have pretty well succeeded in rewriting the art books (the respectable books, that is; they are well aware that what the academicians write won't affect the future), it is becoming increasingly difficult to discern the role of content in the arts of the past. The core of this book, therefore—the three chapters that follow—will be devoted to a reinterpretation of Western painting from Giotto to Rouault with the emphasis on *content*. I shall try to show that the present deification of formal values, far from being a unique development, has been a recurrent historical phenomenon—in its moderate phases, perhaps, the phenomenon by which art manages endlessly to renew itself.

The Epilogue, like this Prologue, will be in a more personal vein, and will attempt to plot the direction which the coming revolt against Formalism is likely to take.

Rouault's "Two Prostitutes." Expressive content in art without sacrifice of formal values. Their "ugliness," the Catholic artist's way of scoring the degradation of the human spirit, resulted in "beauty."

PART TWO [A]

Secularization of the Image:

Giotto to Rembrandt

Sixth Century "Head of Christ." Mosaic, Ravenna. "The story has been completely transformed into pageantry . . . all human, arbitrary and subjective elements suppressed . . . the style solemn, pompous and abstract." —Hauser

PART TWO [A]

Secularization of the Image:

Giotto to Rembrandt

The Renaissance and its painters occupy a wide niche in the educated layman's mind. To talk knowingly of the Mycenaeans, the Sassanids or the Burgundians one must tiptoe into the hush-hush world of scholarship, and once there the going is uncertain: we are not dispassionate or devout enough to be sure of our terms. But the Renaissance is our world. As early as Giotto, the "personality" of the artist puts us at ease—and already we see manifested in his painting that struggle between expressive content and formalism which is our particular concern. Giotto was the end-product of two antithetical ways of looking at the world; resolving their strains, he opened the gates to our own. But first, a backward glance at the forces that shaped him. . . .

Byzantine, Romanesque, Gothic

Early Christian or Byzantine art resembles the Modern (or Formalist) in its dehumanized grandeur, its lack of interest in appearances and objects, its emphasis on texture and flat patterns, its substitution of style for emotion. Like ours it was the expression of the world viewed as a mystery and doomed to imminent material destruction. It differs from ours in having an overlay of communicative content based on a centuries-old tradition of accepted beliefs.

Byzantine art sprang from the world-despairing philosophy of Plotinus, who had suggested ways of "de-materializing" the world, and whose followers rejected empirical knowledge. The artists who practised this dematerialization were decorators—sometimes sublime decorators. It was not their function to add anything new to the accepted iconographies. For centuries, in fact, they were "directed" in the exercise of their craft by the priesthood of the Imperial Byzantine Court. "They had a scale of values of their own in which the costliness and rarity of the materials employed and the difficulties in manipulating them ranked high." [1]

The very technique of mosaic was unsuited to the transmission of a

■

[1] *Byzantine Painting* by André Graber, New York, Skira, 1953.

Byzantinism Today, I. Picasso's "Portrait of Kahnweiler" in the severe style of Analytical Cubism reflects deeper parallelism of two ages—rejection of the world of appearances and human values for de-personalized abstraction. Joseph Scharl's "Head of Christ" is successful translation from mosaic to paint of frontal Byzantine style itself.

content embodying human values or celebrating the world of nature. The setting of *tesserae* in cement made expressive drawing difficult—even if it had been considered desirable. Color was employed schematically to stand for certain principles or personages. The relation of these colors was conceived in abstract, musical terms. Distortions of perspective, causing the figures in the background to loom larger than those in the foreground, reflect a sense of the unreality of earthly appearances. The eyes stare hypnotically. The faces are not personalized. Christ, represented in frontal grandeur, is Himself the High Priest, the King-Emperor.

It is curious that an art as powerful and original as the Byzantine lay forgotten in the squat basilicas for over a thousand years, but it is not strange that our age rediscovered it and values it highly. In the choir of San Vitale, the masterpiece of Byzantine art, the basic forms of modern formalism—geometric and biomorphic abstraction [2]—are prefigured in all their primitive glory. The intricately patterned robes of Theodora's retinue are a foreshadowing of the faceted surfaces of Analytical Cubism at its most complex and severe. The stylized clouds and mountains surrounding Moses on Mt. Sinai bloom with more than a suggestion of the handsome "free

■

[2] See pages 129-131.

Byzantinism Today, II. Gottlieb's handsome stained-glass façade for the Milton Steinberg House indicates, by its non-communicative pictograms, the affinity between today's Non-objectivism and symbolic decorativeness in which Byzantine art ended after all image-making had been officially banned.

forms" of Miró and Gorky. The deliberate use at Torcello of empty spaces as a means of artistic expression was to be reinvoked, though in drier, more linear terms, by Malevich and Mondrian. The first mosaic-like façade of modern times has been designed by an American Non-objectivist who uses as his media two of the favorite Byzantine materials—"costly metals, precious stones, polished glass"—so long ago appropriate to an art that dematerialized the human while reducing the personality of the artist to that of a selector of color values.[3]

It has been said that it took as much genius to forget man in Byzantium as it did to discover him on the Acropolis. There is no reason to doubt it.

∎

[3] The lead-webbed stained-glass exterior wall of the Milton Steinberg House in New York was designed by Adolph Gottlieb in 1953-4. Commenting on it in *Art News*, the Non-objectivist magazine, Dorothy Gees Seckler wrote: "The congregation, which would never have chosen this design, *accepted an artistic result ordained by respected authorities*." (My italics.) In this respect, modern formalism followed Byzantine precedent. In another respect it did not. "Gottlieb is too forthright," Miss Seckler noted, "to disguise the fact that [in his selection of the design] esthetic considerations came first. The panel associated with Yom Kippur is a case in point . . . He first made the line and then decided on an interpretation." In Constantinople and Ravenna the artist followed the instructions of God's earthly intermediaries in choosing his symbols.

But we must not lose sight of the fact that this was the art of a disciplined caste subservient to Authority and speaking to the people only in accents of grave warning or unearthly pomp. Even this communicative phase of Byzantine art was shortlived. San Vitale was consecrated in 547. In 727 all representation in art was officially banned and concentration on the play of geometric and floral motives took over, merging with the already encroaching decorative arts of Islam.

Only in the monasteries, suppressed but not wholly extinguished by the Emperor who wished to keep the priesthood his vassals and sacred art a means of maintaining his absolute authority, were the monks still turning out popular icons with a remnant of pagan sensuality or decorating manuscripts with an irrepressible emphasis on natural forms. It was to the monasteries that Charlemagne turned when he tried, in the Eighth Century, to revive the humanistic ideals of antiquity. There was not by this time, even among the monks, anyone left in the West who could still represent a body plastically. When Charlemagne failed, the Dark Ages became for a time even darker.

No wonder that Romanesque art, when it sought again in the Tenth and Eleventh Centuries to portray the human body three-dimensionally, relied at first on simple, stylized, geometrical forms. It began as a conservative art, this first expression of modern Western man, nurtured by the aristocracy and the feudal bishops and running to symbols of power. Its architecture of cubic forms impressed with a sense of military security. Its first sculptures and paintings sought like the Byzantine to induce a solemn but vague sense of religious acceptance. Only the ornamentation of capitals and the illumination of manuscripts begin to writhe with an animal vitality new to the hieratic canons of the past centuries.

Romanesque and Gothic merge in the Eleventh Century as harmoniously as the towers of Chartres. The fantasy and overstatement of the Romanesque pillar with its fabulous monsters emerge from the undifferentiated stream of decoration into the great dramas of the Last Judgment and the Passion in which the whole community is brought to trial for condemnation or acquittal. The individual participants, in the great portals of Autun and Moissac, impress themselves upon us by the most inventive devices of facial distortion and exaggerated gesture. Vision, fed by growing popular enthusiasm, replaces dogma. The rituals, which had been developed by the clergy to a point of subtlety beyond human comprehension, give way to the miracle plays. The fortress-like Romanesque abbey yields to the soaring Gothic cathedral in whose building the whole people joyously participates. In protest against the calcification of Christianity and the remoteness of the clergy, St. Francis of Assisi, with his creed of poverty, inspires the people to look to nature itself for symbols of purity and to the brotherhood of the birds and the trees for a realization of the value of life in God's world. Simultaneously a passion for learning, for intellectual understanding and encyclopedic knowledge initiated the founding of universities and the much broader dissemination of rediscovered legendry on portal and stained glass.

Malraux, who approves or at least accepts the anti-human foundation

Sculptured figures from the Autun tympanum. Expressive content returns to Western art and reaches heights in late Romanesque, early Gothic period. The anonymous artisan who spoke for a believing community made every facial expression, gesture and fold of drapery convey his emotional involvement.

of modern Formalism, nevertheless asserts that Christianity's supreme discovery in art was that the portrayal of a fully human woman (the Gothic Virgin) had a stronger emotive appeal than idealization or symbolism or abstraction. "Every Christian face," he notes,[4] "is marked by a great tragedy, and the finest Gothic mouths seem like scars that life has made." The stone saints of Chartres and Rheims assume life, become particular sufferers. The psychology of God-made-man in a world where *everyone* is valued replaces the abstract symbolism of the Byzantine Emperor in the guise of an aloof Redeemer. And Malraux, who elsewhere defines a painter as "primarily one who loves pictures," is forced to admit that this art in which the artist "aimed at truth not art," and at Crucifixions not "finer" than others but "more Christ-like," achieved intensities and expressive heights never scaled in the Renaissance or after.

With Christianity becoming after eleven centuries a mass religion, it followed that sculpture and painting should become not private but popular arts. The essence of the Gothic style is its universality. In place of ritualistic dogma it values moral content. Nominalism is a democratic philosophy. In art, everything is humanized. Hauser points out [5] that the Romanesque Christ could not be shown tortured or humiliated since divine sublimity and physical agony were incompatible in the mind of the ruling class. The Gothic Christ is Everyman and His sufferings were appreciated by a world that no longer accepted its burdens fatalistically.

The dynamism of the Gothic is a consequence of the tension produced by the other-worldly spiritualism of Christianity and the developing emphasis on man and nature. In the cathedral and the sculpture which adorned it this dynamism is manifest. But in painting, the two dominant forms, with their special technical requirements, tended to keep the old somewhat apart from the new. Thus in stained glass, an art form by its nature close to mosaic, the tradition of Byzantine abstraction and symbolism tended to survive as late as the Twelfth and Thirteenth Centuries in the magnificent windows of Chartres. Clearly the solid lead strips and small bits of glass were not adaptable to representation or naturalistic detail. The design had to be left flat. And the craftsmen, like the Impressionists seven centuries later, tended to think in terms of the over-all effect produced at a distance—juxtaposing red and blue fragments, for example, to create a royal purple. Nevertheless, the use of color, to create an effect not of geometric subtlety but of emotional warmth, is in line with the Gothic spirit.

The reduced wall-space of the Gothic cathedral allowed little space for painting as we know it. But the illuminated book, in contrast to stained glass, witnessed an imaginative fancy based on visual delight in flowers and climbing foliage as well as a naturalism of content that foreshadowed the Italian Renaissance. Landscape begins to replace the solid gold background. Such secular subjects as a feast or a boar-hunt are painted with an obvious relish for action, facial emotion and the contributory lifelikeness

■

[4] *The Psychology of Art* by André Malraux, New York, Pantheon, 1950.
[5] *The Social History of Art* by Arnold Hauser, New York, Alfred Knopf, 1951.

Villeneuve "Pietà." As late as the Fifteenth Century, Gothic spirit survived in "backward" areas beyond the pale of Renaissance formalism. Rhythm through which feeling is conveyed keeps realistic portraiture of donor and articulate anatomy of the Christ from clashing with symbolic haloes and transcendental gold background.

of the wart on the nose or the bird in the thorn. An emphasis on the feminine is felt for the first time in Christian art.

Giotto: The Spirit Made Flesh

In the painting of Giotto, the awakening Renaissance's desire for naturalism and dramatic story-telling had not gone so far as to preclude a Gothic concern for transcendental content. Contemporaries were said to be astounded by Giotto's fidelity to nature but we are impressed by the economy of his means. Italian painting, which had come out of Byzantine formalism and was to remain there, especially in conservative Siena, for a long time after Giotto's death, took visible shape on the walls of Assisi and Padua.

Giotto for the first time expressed religious content in terms of visual actuality. The lyricism of his "Sermon to the Birds" is made possible by the very fact that St. Francis' story was too fresh to have become encrusted with ritual. It permitted free, informal interpretation. In the great cycle of paintings at Padua, the story of Christ is told in terms of human values and these values are conveyed by human forms. Mary watches the Ascension not in ecstasy but with sorrow. In the "Pietà," the eyes of every participant are focussed on the body of Christ. Every gesture, every expression, every fold of drapery conveys sorrow. The landscape, barren, almost blasted, contributes to the mood. Even the angels weep uncontrollably. Similarly, on the cheeks of Giotto's crucified Christ, real tears are falling.

Giotto's "Lamentation over Christ" (Pietà). Everything in this fresco from the asymmetric composition, bare mountain slope and leafless tree to the heavily bowed mourners and inconsolable angels conveys grief.

In spite of this spiritual content, then, there is apparent something wholly un-Gothic, something that foreshadows five centuries of realism in Giotto's painting. The figures are less individualized than those of the Autun tympanum, more idealized than the saints of Rheims. These for the first time are *figures in space,* almost sculptural masses, and only Giotto's compassion, true to the ideals of Gothic thought, gives them tragic meaning. Giotto himself, the friend of Dante and the follower of St. Francis, was no materialist, but the materialism of commercial Florence begins to be felt in his world. Florence wanted to be shown not mysteries but its own fleshly image. The classicism of the Humanists was yet to come, but Giotto at Padua previsions their belief in the innate dignity of Man.

Pisanello's "Vision of St. Eustace." Rich in content, but content of nature and finely observed detail rather than of religious feeling inspired by its subject, this Quattrocento lyric carries the mediaeval love of pageantry just short of Renaissance formalism.

The Gothic, a frail wisp of the Gothic, stays alive in the pious art of Lorenzo Monaco and Fra Angelico, and in Siena where the courtly and religious traditions of the Middle Ages ran deeper than at Florence, but it is the *objective,* middle-class character of Giotto, the Florentine burgher, that survives into the Quattrocento, and most triumphantly in the sculpture of Donatello and the painting of Masaccio. The painting of the preceding century had been wholly within the lengthening shadow of Giotto. In the early part of the secular-minded Fifteenth a premium on "originality" begins to be felt. Pisanello's charming "Vision of St. Eustace" is remarkable *historically* for the technical skill lavished on its individual figures, but otherwise for the Gothic spirit of its religious images, a world of phenomena, natural and miraculous, testifying in this very diversity and in the loving care with which the artist renders it, to God's grandeur. Only in the pessimistic Christian painting of Hieronymus Bosch at the end of the Quattrocento are objects rendered again with such a lavish fancy, but the Dutch master's diabolism was an isolated phenomenon, without artistic issue until the coming of the Surrealists in our day.

The Quattrocento: Masaccio's Naturalism

There was in Pisanello's art such a primitive poetry as is to be found only at the birth of a world. The same may be said of such brilliant eccentrics as Paolo Uccello and Piero di Cosimo, who blended admirably the Gothic spirit of illuminated legend with the "modern" worship of perspective. Both elements are present to some degree in Donatello and Masaccio, but the emphasis in these great revolutionaries is so profoundly on nature that the spiritual survives only as an expressive force conveying individuality. Thus Donatello's Hebrew prophets in their anachronistic Gothic niches on Giotto's Campanile at Florence—the bald, slack-mouthed one modelled in such a way as to convey the heavy dignity of a Roman senator, the "Jeremiah" in contrast suggesting a restless energy with his pursed lips, tightened neck muscles and wiry hands gripping disorderly folds of drapery. In Masaccio's "Crucifixion" one is less impressed by the religious content of the picture, though it is rendered with considerable feeling, than by the manifold illusions the artist has created. Perspective has turned the flat wall of Santa Maria Novella into a palpable *space*, complete with jutting pilasters, concave medallions and receding barrel-vault. This three-dimensional effect is created by foreshortening, especially of the coffers in the ceiling; by placing the actors in this artificial stage-set some inside and some outside the "vault"; but especially by means of the artist's supreme technical discovery, *chiaroscuro*, by means of which he models the figures in variations of light and shadow so that their features simulate the eye's illusion of luminous plastic masses rather than bodies encompassed by the linear formula that Giotto and his successors relied on. From the use of such methods, a modern historian of art observes, we receive a vision of the world "in which there is nothing mean or ignoble, where *regardless of whether the subject means anything in itself or not* [my italics] the spectator realizes with heightened awareness the potential power and essential dignity of the human spirit." [6]

It was in company with their friend the architect and sculptor Brunelleschi, third of the great triad of "progressive" Quattrocento artists, that Masaccio and Donatello made a discovery that determined the outlook not only of their art but of the art of five centuries to come. It was a discovery that was predetermined by the general loss of faith that had swept over Europe in the early fourteen-hundreds. They discovered the art—and with it absorbed at least something of the outlook—of classical antiquity. Donatello and Brunelleschi went to Rome and actually dug for medallions and small figures in the ruins. From these classic remains, with their close observation and emulation of nature, both artists found a substitute for the

■

[6] *The Harper History of Painting* by David M. Robb, New York, Harpers, 1951.

Masaccio's "Trinity with Virgin, St. John and Donors." The spiritual content still conveyed expressively, but conflicting with the artist's interest in creating an illusion of perspective out of irrelevant architectural props.

religiously expressive linear system of the past, which had degenerated, as the power behind it lost credence, into triviality. With this weapon, which made man once more the measure (and the measurer) of all things, Masaccio created his nude "Adam and Eve," endowing their expulsion from Eden with the drama of a lost (classical?) paradise; and Donatello, in the almost content-less and abstract rhythms of his "Singing Gallery" relief related the individual body for the first time since the pre-Christian era to the classical norm. No wonder that Vasari said of Donatello's work that "life seems to move within the stone." Or that Leonardo, looking back to the painter who was his ancestor and the ancestor of almost every Western painter until Cézanne, exclaimed that "Masaccio showed by the perfection of his work how those who took as their standard anything other than nature were wearying themselves in vain."

The Quattrocento: Piero's Formalism

The painting of the great and various artists of the latter half of the Fifteenth Century is characterized by a religious content almost devoid of religious conviction. It is significant that Filippo Lippi, the monk who seduced a nun and was indicted for forgery, never lost face either in the

Medicean court or before the Church. Ghirlandaio's sumptuous Biblical frescoes were conceived more as settings for the introduction of a court favorite or mistress than as aids to worship. Michelangelo was incensed by the patent spiritual insincerity of Perugino's religious pictures but Perugino's generation was not. The pageantry of Benozzo Gozzoli, the antiquarian spirit of Mantegna, the athleticism of Signorelli reflected without provoking protest the preoccupations of the Renaissance. It is noteworthy that the subject—if indeed there was a subject—of Antonio Pollaiuolo's epoch-making engraving of nude swordsmen has been forgotten. Botticelli,

Pollaiuolo's engraving of nude swordsmen. Wonderfully inventive and controlled study of arrested motion signalizing the Renaissance artist's growing interest in problems of form for their own sake.

it is true, experienced a late "conversion" to Christianity as a result of listening to Savonarola's fiery denunciations of Catholic degradation, but it is Botticelli's linear classicism, the nostalgic expressions of his allegorical heroines, that we remember. In his feeble "religious" pictures we feel that the tenuous style, so well suited to the content of the Medicean fables, has assumed an impossible burden. "In resorting to symbolism as an aid to establishing meaning," Robb well observes, "Botticelli signalized the final discarding of quattrocento unselective factualism as the ultimate criterion in the evaluation of experience and revealed the need of a new tradition."

That tradition had already been foreshadowed in the dazzling white light and mysteriously reticent figures of Piero della Francesca. The true heir of Masaccio, judged as a carrier of the formal revolution of Florentine realism, Piero is an enigmatic figure in his role as a religious painter. The tremendous vogue of this artist in our time requires explanation. Since Aldous Huxley's celebrated essay of 1929 on the "Resurrection" (*The Greatest Picture in the World*) Piero's reputation has grown until today it towers over his century. The two most popular paintings in the London National Gallery were recently voted to be Piero's "Baptism" and his "Nativity." Yet, fifty years after his death, this artist's masterpiece, the frescoes depicting the Story of the True Cross in Arezzo, had been forgotten and was falling into disrepair. A hundred years after their painting Vasari could write that Piero was "the first geometrician of his time" but that his importance as a painter lay in his "copying things as they really are." The centuries that followed didn't even give him credit for that. Yet now it is Berenson, forerunner of the Formalist aesthetic,[7] who holds up Piero as the prototype of

Piero della Francesca's "Resurrection." Presented with a frontality and impassivity reminiscent of the Byzantine masters, Christ's awe-inspiring presence appeals to us for its abstract monumentality and seeming lack of emotion.

the universal artist the purpose of whose art is to *be* rather than to represent. What appeals especially to our time in Piero is his ability (the century before us would have called it inability) to paint the Christian story with exactly the same detachment as he paints a marble façade or the portrait of one of his murderous patrons. That, at any rate, is what many modern critics read into his work.

■

[7] See page 132.

Our passion for the abstract is satisfied by Piero's procedure, building forms out of geometrical theorems (he was the author of several learned treatises on perspective) and using color as Juan Gris, the Cubist, was later to claim that he used it, to construct an architecture of volumes on one plane. Piero's modern biographer, Roberto Longhi, pointed out as early as 1929 the startling resemblance between the apparition of a distant town in the Arezzo frescoes and Cézanne's landscapes, built out of only slightly less differentiated cubes of color. Nor can those who consider Mondrian's geometricism worth while fail to be impressed with Piero's mania for measurement.

Longhi also noted that in the "Flagellation of Christ" at Urbino, Piero created out of a mathematical dream such an architecture as Brunelleschi and Alberti at their most inspired never realized; and he asserted triumphantly that for the first time in painting an artist had laid as much stress on the intervals between forms as on the forms themselves.[8] What impresses me more in this picture, however, is the religious content—the correspondence of the figures moving about through these "perfect voids" to the message they are intended to convey. Masaccio's elaborate architectural setting in the Santa Maria Novella "Crucifixion" was still only a setting; the Christian drama remained primary. But in Piero's picture the Flagellation is *not* the principal focus of interest. What drama there is, is in the impassive confrontation of young Oddantonio da Montefeltro, soon to be assassinated, by his ministers. The scourging of Christ in the distant left background may be regarded as the completion, by sculptural figures, of a demonstration of interlocking architectural lines, planes and volumes. Christ's body is seen to be an integral part of the column to which He is tied and the complement of the classic statue surmounting it. No emotion, hardly even any physical *movement,* is discernible in any of the figures. Yet the religious content of this picture—the content that for the Formalists is irrelevant or non-existent—may have lain for the artist precisely in the removal of Christ's agony to an antechamber and its setting, like that of some legendary event in a cameo, in the framework of a decorative miniature. Piero, despite the insistence of those modern critics who would claim him as an abstractionist, was a religious man with a sure touch in the rendering of spiritual emotion. The gestures of the three figures in his "Crucifixion" at Borgo San Sepolcro are proof enough of that. But by the time Piero came to paint his masterworks, the "Resurrection," the Urbino "Flagellation" and the Arezzo cycle, the artist had lived too long in the cynical princely courts of Italy, observing at first hand the criminal conduct of the Papacy and its representatives abroad, not to be sensible to this mockery of Christ's teachings, and to elect to comment on it, however obliquely, in his painting. What did the torture of Christ mean to Oddantonio and his ministers? The answer is in their blank faces, staring out of the picture as into a mirror. Piero was too good an artist and, I suspect, too good a Christian, to be satisfied with reproducing the events of the New Testament as Pinturicchio or Perugino was, in gilded pageantry or

■

[8] *Piero della Francesca* by Roberto Longhi, London, 1930.

Piero della Francesca's "Flagellation of Christ." Did formalism dictate the subordination of the religious content to the background, mere resolution of an essay in architectural perspective? Or were the three patrons given top-billing as a subtle rebuke to the hypocritical values of the times?

saccharine pantomime.[9] Is it beyond the realm of possibility that Piero chose the obscure mediaeval legend of the adventures of the wood of the Cross as the subject for his mural masterpiece precisely because it reflected the remoteness of true Christianity from his time? In any event there was here revealed a world of primitive poetry and religious innocence in the dawn of the Christian era before corruption set in.

The High Renaissance

Everyone has remarked that on the threshold of the High Renaissance there is discernible a shift of attention from the work of art to the personality of the artist. We know next to nothing about Piero. We know a very great deal about Leonardo. Leonardo's early paintings, such as the "Adoration of the Magi" and the "Virgin of the Rocks," still reflect something of the Gothic sense of God made manifest in a comprehensive knowledge of nature, but already psychological interest is coming to the fore. Scientist

■

[9] Sir Kenneth Clark, with whose book on Piero I was not familiar at the time of this writing, thinks that the "Flagellation" symbolizes the tribulations of the Church; the Infidels captured Constantinople in 1453, approximately the picture's date.

and atheist that he was, Leonardo treated his religious themes as human anecdotes, bringing out first, by the geometric relationships and gestures of his figures, and later by the play of light on their features, the meaning of their dramas. Thus the "Last Supper," with its Apostles in various attitudes expressive of real or imagined guilt, is a monumental essay in love betrayed, and "St. John the Baptist" primarily a study of sexual ambiguity. But in all Leonardo's pictures, characteristically unfinished or fragmentary, the real protagonist is the artist himself, independent of the Church, alienated from society. It is significant that Leonardo was the first man to regard a work of art as the property of the artist, carrying his "Mona Lisa" to France with him and refusing to part with it even after it had been bought by the King of France. Undoubtedly he regarded the portrait as autobiographical. In

Titian's "Sacred and Profane Love." Here, as in Raphael, the High Renaissance ideal of style for its own sake reaches a pinnacle. "The subject as such counts for little or nothing . . . in making the content of the picture a pictorial rather than a literary experience Titian followed the example of Giorgione." —Robb

any event, Christian culture had disintegrated to such an extent by this time that the concept of art as the community's property or God's, and of the artist as simply a medium for representing the divine, had given way to our own. The meaning of the work lay within itself, to be interpreted perhaps by the small circle of Latinized élite, but beyond the comprehension of the "philistine" public.

Leonardo was the friend and confidant of princes. Raphael and Titian were the first artists to become great lords themselves. They painted their secular allegories in churchly palaces but consulted no one except their Humanist friends on questions of content. Since the Popes of the High Renaissance were seeking to glorify themselves rather than God through art, the religious images could be (and were) cold, intellectually self-contained, erudite and completely out of contact with the people. In place of the Quattrocento's emphasis on the concrete, the direct, the accidental, this art expressed physical and intellectual superiority. Although, as Hauser points out wryly, we now praise it for the "universality of its appeal," it was actually "dedicated to the solution of sublimated formal problems."

Michelangelo's "Last Judgment" (detail). Religious content expressed in terms of the artist's personal reaction to the fate of spiritual values. Michelangelo's sense of his own deep involvement is underscored by his anguished self-portrait in the guise of St. Bartholomew's flayed skin.

Michelangelo and the Religious Revival

Michelangelo carried the independence of the artist several steps further. Hauser notes that he could afford to forego all public honors, titles and distinctions and calls him "the first lonely, daemonically impelled modern with a sense of responsibility for his genius." Michelangelo was also, however, the first of that line of lonely painters—it includes Tintoretto and Greco, Gruenewald and Rembrandt, Rouault and Lebrun—to paint a religious cycle inspired by acute personal experience and opposition to reigning complacencies, spiritual and artistic.

Equally proficient as sculptor and painter, Michelangelo's true masters were Donatello and Masaccio, but in adapting what was plastically essential from each and dispensing with everything but the human form, he created in the Sixtine ceiling out of physical realities a spiritual one. The ceiling, and to an even greater degree the frescoes on the end wall and in the nearby Pauline Chapel that completed the cycle, cannot be understood without reference to the religious revival of the Fifteenth and Sixteenth

Centuries. This revival, which assumed the form of Protestantism in Northern Europe, took various shapes in Italy following the burning of Savonarola in 1498. Michelangelo, who admired Savonarola's puritan spirit as much as he admired Dante's, remained a nominal Catholic to the end of his days and this may account in part for the bitterness of his old age. To comment on Christian backsliding as Piero had in the oblique terms of a spectacular calm would have been inconceivable to one of Michelangelo's violent nature. The Sixtine ceiling (1508-12) was as close as the great sculptor ever got to creating in the convention of the day a classic world of idealized humanity, but even there the stress seems less on the Creation than on the Sin and Redemption of mankind. In any case the greatness of this masterpiece lies in the tension between Michelangelo's worship of the sensuous (male) body and his revulsion against the Church's toleration of fleshly values. Michelangelo refused Julius II's admonition to enrich the frescoes with gold, reminding His Holiness that "those who are painted here were poor themselves." But it is ironical that Adrian VI, a Dutchman who became Pope in 1522, was influenced enough by Luther's Theses against the magnificence of the Vatican to contemplate destroying the ceiling which he described as "a hothouse of nudity."

In "The Last Judgment" (1535-40) the heroic reserve of the ceiling frescoes gives way to a profound despair. A vengeful Christ, sending mankind to its terrible doom, reflects the artist's sense of impatience over the Church's inability to rise above the evils of the age as well as his own personal disappointments. Nevertheless the prudish spirit of the Counter Reformation, speaking even through the mouth of the pornographic blackmailer Aretino, was shocked by the nudity of the figures more than by their exaggerated poses, the Baroque hammerblow to Renaissance canons of design. But the significance of the gigantic painting from our point of view is its expression of a religious *conversion* rather than a faith, its modern emphasis on ferocious rage rather than redemption, its quality of *propaganda*. As far back as 1512, watching Rome prepare for war, Michelangelo had written these anti-clerical lines:

> *Here helms and swords are made of chalices:*
> *The blood of Christ sold by the quart:*
> *His cross and thorns are spears and shields, and short*
> *Must be the time ere even His patience cease . . .*
> *For Rome still flays and sells Him at the Court*
> *Where paths are closed to virtue . . .*[10]

In "The Last Judgment" Michelangelo had painted his own face in the guise of the flayed skin of Bartholomew. In the Pauline frescoes of 1543 he painted, in the Crucifixion of Peter and the Conversion of Paul, his own conversion and martyrdom. Crippled by a fall from the scaffold, embittered by the changeable vanities of successive Popes, engaging in mystical con-

■

[10] *The Sonnets of Michelangelo,* translated by J. A. Symonds. Quoted in *Michelangelo: His Life and His Era,* by Giovanni Papini, New York, Dutton, 1952.

versations with Vittoria Colonna and contemplating a holy pilgrimage as a release from his anxieties, he resorted now to autobiography, a statement of personal anguish that though much less extensive than the Sixtine ceiling required eight years to complete. In terms of form, the Pauline murals are more abstract than the Sixtine's and their over-all scheme is more generalized. Michelangelo was in his old age now and one is not surprised to learn that his pessimism led him to accept Luther's concept of the Divine Blood as the sole purifier of sin. In several sonnets of this period, moreover, Michelangelo repudiates art itself as both a distraction from the life of the spirit and an escape.

Tintoretto: Religion as Metaphor

How different is the religious painting of Tintoretto, Michelangelo's great Venetian contemporary! Tintoretto seeks not to indict mankind but to assist in his reformation by the contemplation of Christianity conceived as a spiritual poem. The poem is woven of human bodies moving freely through space with the rhythm of superhuman athletes and bathed in quicksilver. "The drawing of Michelangelo and the coloring of Titian" was the eclectic inscription on Tintoretto's studio wall, but it serves to connote his technical background rather than the inner meaning of his world. Tintoretto's world is not that of the Sixtine ceiling with its classic forms expressing youthful perfection and power, nor of "The Last Judgment" with its cry for redemption amid despair; nor is it Titian's world of sensual affirmations and epic mythology; nor yet Veronese's sunbathed opulence giving to religious subjects a wholly secular content.[11] Tintoretto's "Last Supper" is neither devout nor anecdotal nor psychological; it is a timeless ritual dominated by the mystery of the Eucharist. His great "Crucifixion" of 1565 in San Rocco shows Christ's death as a lonely spectacle taking place above an unconcerned world of warriors and artisans. The keynote—as in all Tintoretto's pictures with their generalized, floating forms and their eery light—is the mystery of the event, and this is in line with the Counter Reformation's stress on religion as a personal revelation and in the style of its fanatical saints—Loyola, Theresa of Avila, Borromeo and John of the Cross. The overstraining of the forms indicates a fear that the formal world of the Renaissance cannot encompass the lost spiritual values of the Middle Ages. We are in a theatrical world. We do not doubt the sincerity of Tintoretto's religious experience, but we are uncomfortably aware that the gods have become actors, their world a stage, and ourselves guests at the mystery rather than participants.

Only two painters are able to maintain the conviction of the religious

■

[11] Questioned by the Inquisition on why he painted more figures in his "Last Supper" than tradition required, Veronese answered that additional ones were called for to fill additional space. The question has been seen as pre-figuring the Church's role in fixing the Baroque as a rigid academic style, the answer as the first insistence by an artist that subjective, formal considerations are primary and the artist's prerogative alone.

Tintoretto's "Crucifixion" (detail). Religious content transmuted into drama of mythological poetry with indirect lighting. Desperate experimentalism of our time was anticipated in Tintoretto's efforts to recapture spiritual expression through such devices as hanging figurines in shadow boxes and illuminating them with candles.

experience in this time of Jesuitical compromises. Lorenzo Lotto, a non-conforming psychological painter whose art is as personal as that of Titian is typical, managed it by going back directly to the Scriptures, interpreting the Christian legend in terms of his own yearning for communion with God. Berenson, his biographer, contrasts Lotto's search for the inner life with Titian's indifference to what his *dramatis personae* think or feel. "A constant wanderer over the face of the earth, he [Lotto] could not shut his eyes to its ruin nor make a rush for a share in the spoils. The real Renaissance, with all its blithe promise, seemed over and gone. Lotto like many of his noble countrymen turned to religion for consolation. But not to the official Christianity of the past, nor to the stereotyped Romanisms of the nearer future." But Lotto, an evangelist, almost a Lutheran, "in a country in which a rigid and soulless Catholicism was daily strengthening its hold," died in poverty and neglect, not to be appreciated for over three hundred years. It remains to be seen how El Greco, the other great religious individualist of the time, managed to maintain his conviction by resorting to effects of distortion and light quite beyond the pale of Renaissance naturalism.

Gruenewald's Unrestrained Emotionalism

With the art of Greco, and of Gruenewald who died a few years before Greco's birth, we reach the pinnacles as well as the conclusion of that epoch of religious painting which began when Michelangelo witnessed the martyrdom of Savonarola and Botticelli hurled his Medicean allegories on the pyre.

The "Crucifixion" of Gruenewald's Isenheim altarpiece differs from Tintoretto's not merely in inviting our participation but in *forcing* it. It is as if this artist deliberately gathered together all the elements of mediaeval involvement and Renaissance plasticity, and then, despairing that even this combination would be enough to waken the sleeping conscience of a complacent world, went directly to the hospital ward of the monastery for which he was painting his masterpiece. That hospital ward, we now know, specialized in cases of venereal disease and leprosy. Christ's body, no less than those of the pathological dwarf and the gruesome monsters in the accompanying "Temptation of St. Anthony," is embellished with every horror of corruption that flesh can wear. The skin, covered with sores, is an ashen grey turning green. The feet are twisted by the spike. The nailed hands writhe convulsively, as do those of the Magdalen and the fainting Virgin; while John the Baptist points almost mockingly over the inscribed words HE MUST GROW AS I DECREASE.

Gruenewald's diabolism has been compared to that of Bosch who painted at almost the same time his famous "Temptation of St. Anthony," now in Lisbon. But Bosch's world seems literary, almost childishly mechanical in its fantasies of horror, compared with Gruenewald's, and the Dutch artist's "Christ Bearing His Cross," with its lynch-mob like capitalists in a Communist cartoon, is unrelieved by any Christian sense of human suffering as a stage in the achievement of divine love. Gruenewald worked with Duerer after 1492, but Gruenewald's unrestrained emotionalism bears

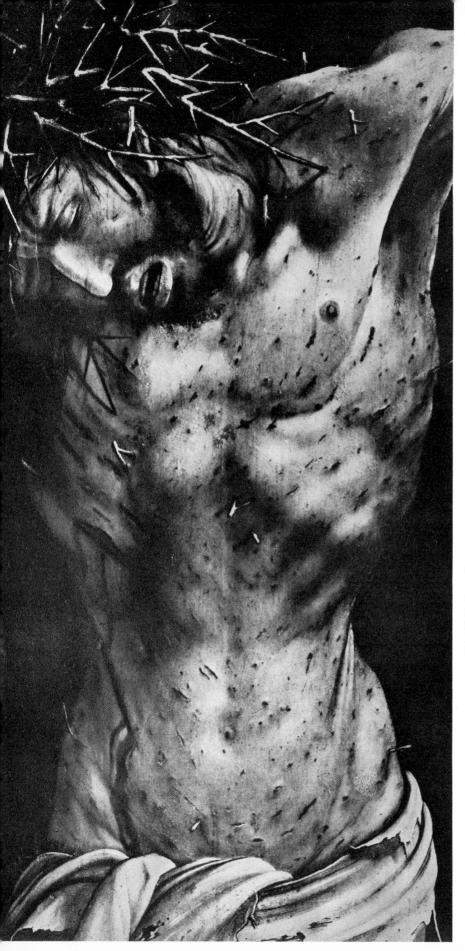

Gruenewald's "Crucifixion" (detail). Realistic only in its means, this masterwork of an inspired mystic foreshadows the art of Van Gogh and Kokoschka, Orozco and Lebrun.

the same relation to the great engraver's preoccupation with death and the macabre as Orozco's visionary images in our time to the popular engravings of Posada.[12] Was Gruenewald a realist? Only in the sense that visions, as in all great art, are compounded of observed nature as well as emotional insight. Gruenewald may be considered more truly the father of modern Expressionism from Van Gogh and Ensor to Kokoschka and Soutine than the ancestor of those Surrealists who claim him as theirs. One need only compare Gruenewald's "Temptation of St. Anthony" with Max Ernst's (which draws upon the earlier painter's horrors for much of its detail) to be aware of the difference between an intellectual cleverness which conveys no real terror, and the hell of the spirit. The Surrealists claim to paint "automatically" as in the manner of children or madmen, but we rarely have a sense in their art, as in Gruenewald's, that they are drawing upon subconscious levels of fear and evil common to all men. The difference, perhaps, is that Gruenewald's intention is to communicate, on the basis of an accepted symbolism and by the depths of his penetration to shocking pits of human fallibility, rather than to shock the spectator by an arbitrary marshalling of invented hobgoblins.

Picasso's biographer, Christian Zervos, in an essay on Gruenewald dedicated to the Surrealist poet Paul Eluard, seeks to define in general terms what it is in the German master that appeals to us so particularly. He singles out Gruenewald's economy of means, his rejection of easy solutions

Bosch's "Christ Bearing His Cross." Ancestor of Surrealism, with an inventive imagination more prodigious than Goya's or Picasso's, this artist appeals to us because of his rejection of a rational world. Is the one he substitutes for it the world of the subconscious mind? Note that the identifiable figures, Christ and Veronica, have their eyes closed.

and his painterly synthesis of line and color; but these are characteristics of good painting in all ages. At only one point does he hint at the reason for Gruenewald's fascination for us. The Isenheim altarpiece, he asserts, satisfies us "so exactly that it seems born of our inquietudes." Gruenewald lived in a time of soul-destroying poverty, fatal plagues and devastating wars that must have seemed well-nigh irreversible by rational means. But

■

[12] See page 106.

the anxiety reflected in his pictures is more than overridden by the rebellious spirit of the artist, and the focus on death by a transfiguring faith.
In comparison, the disasters of our time seem man-made and subject to
amelioration, at least in part, by science. Only charity, a belief in the worth
and continuity of the individual human being, and the will to struggle
with evil—traits certainly not antithetical to the sensibility of the artist
even in a materialistic age—seem lacking. Yet rarely and with little conviction does the Twentieth Century artist reflect anything but the anxiety in
his intellectual automatism, the defeat of the will in his abstractions, the
guilt in his de-humanized monsters.

Greco's Transfigured World

It is interesting to compare the "Resurrection" in the Isenheim polyptych with Piero della Francesca's great painting at Borgo San Sepolcro [13]
and with the "Resurrection" of El Greco in Madrid. Those of us who regard
the heroism of the survivors of Buchenwald or Bataan or Hiroshima as
subject-matter too sentimental even to contemplate might consider the
varieties of comment on human indifference in these three pictures of such
obvious contemporary reference. In Piero's fresco, the Roman centurions
may be taken as embodiments (from left to right) of self-pity, animal indifference, battle fatigue and boredom. They are not so much asleep as
drugged by spiritual sloth; and the appearance of Christ, in keeping with

Gruenewald's "Soldiers of the Resurrection." Expressive content, drawing alike on the Gothic
spirit that survived in the North and on the representational resources of the Renaissance. Even
in this detail of the Isenheim Altarpiece the emotional connotations of writhing hands, unavail-
ing helms and defeated brawn are overwhelming.

the humanistic bias of the Italian Renaissance, is not so much a miracle as
a phenomenon of the will, demanding intellectual courage and integrity to
be grasped, qualities lacking in the Romans of Pilate's day as in the Romans
of Piero's. Gruenewald's soldiers, in contrast, are not indifferent. They are

■

[13] See page 43.

Gruenewald's "Temptation of St. Anthony." Whereas Bosch's elaborately contrived fantasies seem to be saying that man is pretentious and ludicrous when he isn't disgusting—that faith itself is self-deception—Gruenewald's monsters, more convincingly real, suggest that even the diseased and the damned may be saved.

literally bowled over by fear—fear of the unknown, the supernatural, the spiritual. All of them have their faces covered. All turn away from Christ's apparition violently, one covering his face symbolically with the slit-eyed mask of his helmet, one ducking as from a physical blow, the third kneeling

Greco's "Resurrection" (detail). Triumph—over the body, over gravity, over mortality, over death—compellingly expressed in the stretched forms of this soaring apotheosis.

with almost comic haste as if to make an atheist's gamble on a last-minute gesture of religiosity. Christ is indeed an apparition in this picture, radiating light, the head dissolved in light, the movement of body and hands wholly unreal, as if to convey such a message as "This is no time for compromise; accept Me as I am, Spirit entire, or not at all." How different is Greco's conception in which all the soldiers look to the risen Christ, even in the act of brandishing their swords! Not only look, but move; for each of them is caught up in the ecstasy, stripped naked of his earthly raiment, elongated by desire for union, carried round and about in irresistible swirls of movement but always upward. Even the soldier who has been startled so that he falls on his head seems surely destined to embrace the Prophet whose body and expression are the only static elements in the whole flaming whirlpool of ascension. Here nothing is equated with nature or the world. The soldiers are superbly muscled, to be sure, but these are muscles intended for no earthly athletics; they could be the musculature required for flying. Greco's vision, deliberately set off from its frame by arbitrary patches of black, white and pink paint, must be accepted on its own terms as vision. It is abstraction in the deepest sense, abstraction employed to project the artist's sense of spiritual aspiration, of man's body abstracted from its earthly dimensions as he approaches *by struggle* the sublime *stasis* of Man become God.

Greco as a "convert" to Christianity has nothing of the theologically perfunctory in his religious pictures. Professor Robb is not being far-fetched when he calls him a realist whose chief concern was to make spiritual experience as actual as possible in terms of line and color. Thus Greco's portrait of the Cardinal Don Fernando Niño de Guevara in New York emphasizes the inhuman energy of this Grand Inquisitor whose eyes behind their heavy glasses look past the artist, not conceding the possibility "that he was anything but the instrument by which wrongdoing was punished." Similarly does the "View of Toledo in a Storm" (also in New

Greco's "View of Toledo." Whether this picture is thought of as landscape, abstraction or apocalyptic prophecy, the artist does not carry subjectivism to the point of denying humanity. Tiny figures bathing and washing clothes are reminders that life goes on.

York) define content through design. This last of Greco's pictures confers upon landscape alone all the emotional frenzy of the Inquisition—the city implacably gripping the hills, the corpse-gray sky mushrooming with promise of apocalyptic vengeance: Spain that has disavowed its fanatical new saints crucified by Christ's own servants. It is said that Greco in this final period used to sit behind curtained windows in broad daylight the better to "see" the world of his tormented vision. "The glare of day would harm my inner light," he is reputed to have said. Hauser remarks sarcastically that what Greco was looking for would have been visible to an artist of the Middle Ages even in the blaze of noon and sees an era of cranks and psychopaths in the wake of Parmigianino's alchemy, Pontormo's fits of depression, Rosso's suicide and Tasso's insanity. But however historically interesting and true that may be, the fact of Greco's retreat from the visible world detracts nothing from his achievement. His insight always has the accuracy of his memory to fall back on. But it does point up the increasing isolation of the artist and the growing desperation with which he pits himself against a hostile environment, seeking any contrivance to make his art more intense. For the artist without Greco's insight and memory, contrivance was on the way to being an end in itself.

Rembrandt: The World Within

In losing, through the eccentricity of his style, the patronage of a conventional monarch, Greco was fortunate enough to receive that of the Church, whose Spanish branch was still sufficiently provincial and permeated with Counter Reformation mysticism to appreciate his unearthly splendors. Rembrandt, the next great artist of expressive content, was less fortunate. He became the first major painter to find no market for his work at all. This was partly but by no means entirely because of a revolution that had been going on for some time in the technique of painting itself. Titian in his last paintings had anticipated Impressionism, doing away with the Renaissance outlining of forms almost wholly; but Titian was too well established as he approached the age of one hundred to arouse any suspicion that he was being aesthetically subversive. Bravura of brushwork became a major component of Rubens' celebrations of mundane power. Rembrandt's contemporary Frans Hals had struck an even more modern note at the end of his career by painting his "Lady Regents of the Haarlem Poorhouse" with hands so stylized that a few strokes of color had been enough to convey their individuality. Hals, significantly, had lost so many patrons by the time he painted it that he was in the poorhouse himself. His likenesses, as he experimented with formal shortcuts, had become less flattering. One can imagine the Lady Regents consoling themselves by remarking that the poor artist had lost his sense of the "beautiful." And then had come Rembrandt, the outcast, the artist who rejected classical norms of "beauty" entirely, who insisted on making Light the subject of his "Night Watch"; the artist whose religious masterpieces found no place in a Protestant Church that had just condemned Catholic "image worship."

Like the great Peter Bruegel before him, Rembrandt seeks out the eternal in the commonest objects and events of everyday life, investing them, as Bruegel had even his sunbathed harvesters, with mystery. In Rembrandt, it can be anything from an old broom to a glittering helmet, but never is the object unrelated to its user or wearer. Still-lifes were popular in Seventeenth Century Holland, but Rembrandt's are unique not merely for their mystery but for their subtle relationship to life, however dimly suggested, in the background. He draws so much, and so greatly, because he must be in intimate contact with the living world around him. And everything is accepted, whether it is ugly or beautiful, because everything issues from the Creator and so is intimately related.

In this democratic spirit Rembrandt distinguishes himself from most of the great religious painters. All of his pictures except the earliest have a spiritual content, but those with specific Biblical themes often seem to have less than those depicting a purely human situation. "The Prodigal Son" is a contemporary parable. But we are less moved by "Christ at Emmaus" than by "Lucrece's Suicide" or even the "Old Woman Cutting Her Nails"—so directly is the Christian *spirit* transmitted into the artist's homely observations. The same phenomenon will be observed in Daumier. Like Rouault in our time, moreover, Rembrandt is most reverent (because most compassionately Christian?) when painting a prostitute. His thematically religious pictures are distinguished by their sympathy for the subjects as suffering human beings—an understanding that perceptibly grows as the artist's fortunes wane, thus increasing their poignancy as autobiography. Christ is not only humble and understanding—he is a poor man, and a Jew.

It is this fusion of the real with the visionary that makes Rembrandt the greatest painter of expressive content the world has ever known, differ-

Rembrandt's "Return of the Prodigal Son" (detail). Artificial light, deep shadow, sagging garments, dramatic relationship of hands and feet employed by the artist for one end alone: the expression of compassion.

entiating him so sharply from his contemporaries and relating him (so movingly in our eyes) to Daumier and Van Gogh, Orozco and Bloom. Coming out of the Baroque tradition, he replaced its theatricalism with a terrible sincerity. Light is never used, as in Tintoretto or Caravaggio, for merely dramatic effect but to define the relation of the inner man to his outer environment. The darkness in his landscapes defines his own feelings. Since the individual for Rembrandt is everything, the mass subjects that appealed to the artists of the Baroque, like the Massacre of the Innocents, held no attraction for him. On the very few occasions when the Dutch did call upon Rembrandt for a major work involving many figures, he responded wholeheartedly and with a psychological penetration into the relationship of such groups, a sympathy for the corporative spirit, that has never been equalled.

Rembrandt's various versions of the "Descent from the Cross" and his "Bathsheeba" have been compared with the paintings of the same subjects by Rubens.[13] Rubens in his early work devoted almost as much attention to the expressive content of a work as to its formal qualities, but as he prospered and turned over more and more of his commissions to assistants, paint quality became a major preoccupation. Rubens' Antwerp "Descent"

Rembrandt's "Old Woman Cutting Her Nails." A subject that in almost any other hands would have been anecdotal and sentimental transformed by the artist's respect for character into an almost heroic symbol.

resounds with beauty, dignity and heroism, three classical requirements of painting that Rembrandt dispensed with when he painted his versions, giving us instead a horribly sagging body, lighted to accentuate its suffering and surrounded by people whose participation in the scene is a function of their involvement in the tragedy. Rubens' "Bathsheeba" in Dresden has been properly described as possessing "feminine charm and painterly bril-

■

[13] *Rembrandt* by Jakob Rosenberg, Cambridge, Harvard University Press, 1948.

liance." Rembrandt's has these *plus* an awe-inspiring revelation of Bathsheeba's *feelings*.

Rosenberg emphasizes also the amazing obsession of Rembrandt with religious subjects in an environment which neither regarded such subjects as any longer relevant nor paid for them. He ascribes this to Rembrandt's embracing, late in life, the Mennonite creed. Mennonism went back to the original and literal content of the Bible, excluding all dogmas, sacraments and ceremonies not instituted by Christ Himself. Mennonites refused to bear arms or to take an oath. They preferred the "poor in spirit" to the "worldly wise and learned" and accepted their brethren in Christ "without any respect to person." Man's heart and conscience were regarded as supreme. Menno said: "Be long-suffering, peaceable, merciful, affectionate and truly humble." A saying of Christ's central to Menno's writings—"Suffer the little children to come unto Me, and forbid them not, for of such is the Kingdom of Heaven"—is the subject of Rembrandt's most famous etching, a subject rarely treated by other Christian artists.

But in the world of the Reformation this artist, who alone saw (in its spirit) that man's miseries gave Christ's sacrifice its meaning, found no place. The Dutch rulers wanted dignified likenesses. The middle class

Rembrandt's "Descent from the Cross." History's most dramatic moment given new dimensions by the artist's concentration on its most easily grasped implications.

wanted picturesque anecdote. The Protestant Church, following Calvin's doctrine that painting should be concerned only with rendering the visible world, had long since ceased to be a patron of the arts. Art dealers, making their first appearance, preferred to make a sure profit with the accepted and scarce pictures of the past. The estrangement of the public from the artist was beginning.

No wonder that Rembrandt took to painting pictures of himself—over and over again, with increasing insight but increasing privacy of communication. The landscape detached from "subject" was almost his invention.

Still-life in his hands became a major art. "Three Trees" is the lyrical complement of the "Three Crosses." The "Flayed Ox" of the Louvre boils with an energy more cosmic than Dr. Tulp and all his anatomy students.

The modern era is in sight. Rembrandt, Malraux rightly says, waged war with all his genius against the world of appearances and a social order in which he saw nothing but a blind wall separating him from Christ. But in his art Rembrandt achieved "a world worthy of Christ." Vermeer and Chardin were about to achieve "a world worthy of painting." In Vermeer's "Love Letter," Malraux admits, "the letter has no importance and the woman none." The same words could be used to describe a typical picture by Gainsborough, Watteau, Poussin, Manet or Matisse.

Rembrandt's "Three Crosses" (etching). The world of the spirit, bathed in its own radiance, presented as the *real* world.

PART TWO [B]

The Search for Simplicity:

The Nineteenth Century

Poussin's "Triumph of Neptune and Amphitrite." With Botticelli, Raphael and Titian this kind of mythological subject came into vogue, but in their treatment of it, the content to some degree still dictated the form. With Poussin, artificiality is deliberately accepted to heighten the composition's formal values.

PART TWO [B]

The Search for Simplicity:

The Nineteenth Century

It was in the same year that Rembrandt's art was being rejected by the burghers of Amsterdam that Poussin, the greatest painter of Seventeenth Century France and the true ancestor of modern Formalism, was leaving Paris for Rome. Poussin, whom Cézanne two centuries later was to "revivify" (in his own words) "upon nature," went to Rome not only to absorb the classical but to escape from a native environment momentarily hostile to it. Poussin had been present when the Luxembourg Palace was being prepared for the installation of Rubens' monumental paintings in honor of Marie de' Medicis. This celebration of sensuous worldly values was not for him nor was there any French artist of the time who could have carried out such a commission. Several years later the French Academy was established, and although Poussin posthumously was to become its hero, in 1648 it sanctioned nothing in art but the then-decadent and bombastic tradition of the Baroque.

Classicism: Poussin to David

Poussin's obsession with logic and order must be appreciated against the background of a century that gave birth to the great philosophers of the rational enlightenment and witnessed revolutionary discoveries in the sciences, especially optics. This was the century of Newton and Descartes. In Spain, Velasquez had already painted his "Surrender at Breda" with its focussing on different degrees of distance, and was about to paint "Las Meninas" with its multiple illusions of mirrors and pictures-within-pictures. As a matter of fact as early as his twenty-first birthday, and before his two visits to Italy, Velasquez had painted a picture that affords a startling parallel to Piero della Francesca's "Flagellation." It was dominated by two very large figures of peasant women preparing food and staring at the beholder. But the ostensible *content* (from which the title "Christ in the House of Martha and Mary" derived) was visible only as a reflection in a mirror in the background! If one were to add that the English were the first to honor Velasquez and that he became the darling of Ruskin and the Royal Academy, it would not be to belittle his genius but to suggest that the formalists of today are most likely to be found hanging over the club mantelpieces of tomorrow.

If Poussin was less factually bemused by the mechanics of vision, he was even more preoccupied with compositional geometry. The fashionable Roman choice of the moment—as between Caravaggio's naturalism and the melodramatic mannerism of the Carracci—did not interest him. He began by drawing from the reliefs in the Arch of Titus and copying the Roman "Aldobrandini Wedding." Then he went to school to those masters of Renaissance formalism, Raphael and Giorgione. He had already written a friend from Roman Nîmes: "The charming girls you will see here will not delight your spirit less than the sight of the beautiful columns of the Maison Carrée." And he added, characteristically: "Things which are perfect must not be regarded hastily, but with deliberation, with judgment and with intelligence." Even in Poussin's early pictures such as the violently tragic "Massacre of the Innocents," the emphasis is on the saving grace of pattern. Later, as in "The Triumph of Neptune and Amphitrite," the content of Poussin's pictures becomes less and less important as he struggles to integrate forms with color, colored forms with landscape, finally nature with space itself. It is significant that one of this artist's last pictures, nominally religious in subject-matter, was entitled "Landscape with St. Matthew." The tiny figure of the Apostle amid classical ruins in the foreground appears to be dictating his memoirs to an angelic secretary.

The century that followed Poussin's death in 1665 was a bad one for art in general and for painting in particular. Rational scepticism is conducive neither to strong beliefs nor fiery rejections. Voltaire is a great figure but a poor poet. The Academy became entrenched in all countries. In France the scene was dominated by Boucher whose insipid classical allegories were designed to stimulate the frivolous tastes and surfeited sensuality of the Courts of the last Louis's. In England the dominant figure was Sir Joshua Reynolds, a politician, flatterer and artistic dictator who did as much as any man to put English painting on the plane of genial characterization and eclectic grace from which it has seldom deviated. As always in such times there were exceptional men who rose above convention to the extent that the times permitted. Watteau's sensibility gave nostalgic distinction to Boucher's set-pieces by using color expressively and by isolating such wistful symbols of forced unreality as the clown. Chardin, a man of the people, with a genius for realistic abstraction comparable to Vermeer's, reflected the virtues of the rising bourgeoisie by painting first genre pictures of a singular chastity and finally still-lives emphasizing purely formal relationships. Hogarth, an illustrator of moral integrity and wit, never quite managed to make the foibles of a dissolute age into images of universal charge.

The age is summed up in the art of Jacques Louis David, the painter of the French Revolution—and Napoleon. For it is David's distinction to have been so fundamentally a child of the Eighteenth Century that he could express nothing of the greatest upsurge of sensibility and libertarianism in history except its doctrinaire cult of the Romans.

David's "Lictors Bringing to Brutus the Bodies of His Sons" (detail). Poussin's formalism, in the hands of an artist without convictions or taste, becoming academicism. Supreme technical skill only underscores the aridity of the content—unexperienced and therefore sentimentalized.

When David painted Brutus he copied Roman sculpture directly. When depicting a bacchante he sent to Rome for an "authentic" coiffure. When he was painting his "Sabine Women" he said: "My purpose in creating this picture was to paint ancient customs with such exactitude that the Greeks and the Romans, seeing my work, would not have found me foreign to their way of living." David had the sensibility of an illustrator but his spirit, that of a go-getter, made him address himself to ever more

Goya's "Why?" (etching-aquatint from *The Disasters of War*). Contemporaneous with David. Expressive content re-enters art again, taking its cue from the nervous style of the French engraver Callot a century earlier. The content—indifference of the exploiter, unending victimization of the common man—creates new forms.

Goya's "Executions of the Third of May, 1808." Expressive content in the grand manner. Every detail, experienced and visualized, distilled into a universally comprehensive pictorial statement, spiritual in the broadest sense. Compare with "Grivitza, 1933" on page 148.

resounding themes. When Napoleon put his foot upon the rights of man, David, who had painted Marat as a martyr and gone to jail for espousing the cause of the fanatical Robespierre, outdid himself in glorifying the arrogant dictator. David's congenital respect for authority is betrayed in his constant use of the word "imitation." "What matters truth," he wrote, "if the attitudes are noble?" And it is the cynicism of this doctrine, coupled with David's prodigious skill in neo-classical dramatic painting, portraiture, and the art of imposing his taste on a whole generation through a new academy, that may account for the esteem in which this frigid painter has been held in France to this day.

Revolutionary Interlude: Goya and Blake

Before coming to the superficially hostile issue of David in Delacroix and Ingres, let us consider at this point an art that seems in its origins somewhat outside the main current of the times but that was to have an incalculable influence on subsequent painting. Not enough is known of the life of Goya to determine with certainty what accounts for the strangely modern duality of this great artist. On the one hand there is the Goya who says "I see only forms that are lighted and forms that are not—planes that are nearer and planes that are far—projections and hollows." (It could be Cézanne speaking of his cones and cylinders!) This was the Goya who carried Velasquez' analysis of atmosphere a step further, who could paint the Duchess of Alba (Maja) nude with a detachment rivalling Manet's and who invented a way of brushing in flat and unmodulated planes that was to inspire the Impressionists.

On the other hand there is Goya the realist, painter of the devastatingly brutal group-portrait of "Charles IV and His Family"; Goya, the expressionist, whose flamboyantly emotional "Shootings of 3 May 1808" says more about the French Revolution and Napoleon than David said in a lifetime; Goya of the "Caprices" and the "Disasters of War," a social reformer fiercely attacking the corruptions of Church and State. This second Goya is the artist who takes up expressive content, concern for humanity and spiritual penetration at the points where Rembrandt had left them.

Like Rembrandt, Goya instinctively felt himself at odds with the dominant church of his day. He painted for this church but his paintings with religious subject-matter are forced, almost insincere. The "Shootings," on the other hand, is deeply religious not only in terms of its protest against un-Christian bloodletting but as an expression of the martyrdom of belief. Venturi [1] calls this painting a masterpiece unexampled in all the history of art by reason of its mobilization of the artist's personality through a force transcending it, "identifying it with the eternal tragedy of human violence . . . a mode of religious feeling." The composition, he adds, "is oblique, in order to accentuate, within the space occupied, the fact of the event. The form is revealed by the light or hidden by the shade, in such a way as to present itself squared, sketched, dynamic, as positive as it is violent. It is

[1] *Modern Painters* by Lionello Venturi, London, 1947.

Hell, and only on a distant height, a church and a house represent the in-difference of nature, to offset the human tragedy." Is it any wonder that we sense in the artificial gaslight and agonized "snapshots" from everyday life in this Spanish painter an "anxiety" that binds his troubled vision of a world in chaos to our own?

It is known that as a young man Goya spent some time in Rome. Legend even has it that he went there as a bullfighter. Over a century before, the great French engraver Jacques Callot had spent much of his short life there, but unlike his fellow-exile and countryman, Poussin, Callot had been an expressive realist. Callot had engraved a series of "Caprices" of his own, and also some plates on war's disasters, and it is not impossible that Goya, like Rembrandt before him, became acquainted with them. It is also more than likely that Goya saw in Rome some of the eerily-lighted *commedia del'arte* paintings of Magnasco, whose world of gypsies, mon-keys, masks and Inquisitorial tortures is reborn in the Spaniard without the fantastical implications of the Italian.

Charles Poore, in his biography of Goya,[2] thinks that it was the painter's deafness that more than anything else led to his invention of that extraordinary "sign-language" by which he managed to convey emotion without resorting to the arabesques, distracting romantic backgrounds, played-out gestures and facial expressions of the art of his time. Malraux, in the introduction to a recent edition of some of Goya's drawings, goes further and speculates that this malady, prefiguring in the artist's mind the possibility of insanity, made him realize that "laughter may express the despair of the condemned better than tears." The French critic observes that the only real face in the "Caprices" is Goya's own. It is true in any event that Goya identified himself with the victims of social injustice and war rather than merely "feeling sorry for them." His manner of drawing with the brush—from the inside out rather than in terms of volumes en-closed by lines—anticipated the sketchy technique of Daumier who was soon to say "You know quite well I can't draw from life!" His world of "masks" pursued by demons would be reborn almost a century later in the carnival symbolism that was Ensor's only way of expressing his reactions to the de-humanizing mass-murder of the First and Second World Wars.

Living in the time of Reynolds, for whose facile portraiture he had contempt, and in an England whose true means of expression has never been graphic, William Blake, unlike Goya, took refuge from the outset in a world of the Imagination. This is the strength and the weakness of his art. It saves him from the limitations of Hogarth. But those "minute par-ticulars" which he rightly called for and which give his poetry its over-powering immediacy, are absent from his gray world of graven shadows.

Blake's acknowledged masters were Michelangelo and Duerer, but he lacks the self-conscious mastery of detail for which the great German is justly renowned and the magisterial summing-up of a great tradition that is so moving in the work of the Italian. One senses uncomfortably in

■

[2] *Goya* by Charles Poore, New York, Scribner, 1939.

Blake's watercolors and engravings something eccentric, constricted, other-worldly in an almost Byzantine way, as if one were contemplating the work of an inspired crank, or of a sane man who had spent most of his life in an asylum. But for all this cramping isolation Blake remains the greatest of English painters and one of the great religious expressionists of any time. His "Job's Despair" is a terrifying image of human degradation that Gruene-wald would have understood. Placing its central figure amid symbolic mourners in a timeless architectural setting, Blake elevates that degrada-

Blake's "Job's Despair." Less expressive than Goya—not so much because of its literary subject as because of the extreme simplification of forms and landscape conceived as symbols.

tion above the merely physical, conferring on it such a dignity as the German painter of the polyptych achieves through successive unfolding layers of experience. The most sympathetic and accurate description of Blake's almost indescribable achievement is that of Roger Fry:

> There assuredly never was a more singular, more inexplicable phenomenon than the intrusion, as though by direct intervention of Providence, of this Assyrian spirit into the vapidly polite circles

of eighteenth-century London. The fact that, as far as the Middle Classes of England were concerned, Puritanism had for a century and a half blocked every inlet and outlet of poetical feeling and imaginative conviction save one, may give us a clue to the causes of such a phenomenon. It was the devotion of Puritan England to the Bible, to the Old Testament especially, that fed such a spirit as Blake's directly from the sources of the most primeval, the vastest and most abstract imagery that we possess. Brooding on the vague and tremendous images of Hebrew and Chaldean poetry, he arrived at such indifference to the actual material world, at such an intimate perception of the elemental forces which sway the spirit with immortal hopes and infinite terrors when it is most withdrawn from its bodily conditions, that what was given to his internal vision became incomparably more definite, precise and clearly articulated, than anything presented to his senses. His forms are the visible counterparts of those words, like *the deep, many waters, firmament, the foundations of the earth, pit* and *host,* whose resonant overtones blur and enrich the sense of the Old Testament.[3]

Classicism: Ingres and Delacroix

Returning to the mainstream of Western painting, the year is 1819 and we are in the Salon at Paris. Goya has come to France where he is to die nine years later. Blake has not yet begun his illustrations to the *Book of Job.* But these artists are not present, either in the flesh of paint or in the spirit. With the advantage of hindsight, if our taste is still determined by the Beaux-Arts of David, we pause before the two pictures that will determine the style of the next fifty years—the styles that count—and we are properly shocked. Géricault's "Raft of the Medusa" confronts Ingres' "Grande Odalisque."

Géricault was to die only five years later at the age of thirty-three but his huge theatrical picture was the herald of Delacroix's full-blown Romanticism. It is improbable that the young artist knew Goya but his painting was in the line of the Spanish artist in one respect. Its point of departure was a scene of topical contemporary interest. The shipwreck was a real one, and in addition it had become a popular symbol of the political incompetence of Louis XVIII. But the picture was condemned by the conservatives less for this than for the fact that it treated common seamen as heroic figures of history. Géricault was a true romantic. "I start a sketch of a woman," he said, "and it comes out a lion." But the aspect of his art that Delacroix seized upon was its apparent re-creation of the mood of the Old Masters out of episodic contemporary material.

Ingres' "Odalisque," in contrast, with its static linear appeal and muted colors, ushered in a century of aesthetic generalization that was to culmi-

■

[3] *Vision and Design,* by Roger Fry. Quoted in *Art Through the Ages* by Helen Gardiner, New York, Harcourt, Brace, 1926.

nate in pure abstraction. Professor Robb compares this famous picture with similar images of nude women from the past. "Unlike Titian," he says, "Ingres was not interested in textures, either pictorial or natural. Unlike Rubens he did not make the figure the symbol of a vigorous and vital humanism . . . nor an immediate re-creation of material presence and appearance in the manner of Goya's nude Maja. Without physical allure or the sensuous appeal of texture and color of pigments, it exists first and foremost as a marvelously integrated *pattern of lines, organized to suggest solid forms in space.*" (My italics.) Ingres' definition of drawing—"To draw

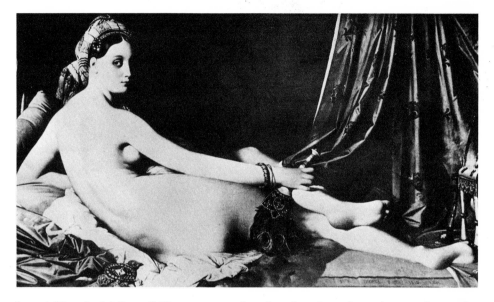

Ingres' "Grande Odalisque." First step toward modern formalism. ". . . the typical case of a form deliberately classical superimposed on a tendentiously romantic content, without the content ever being completely fused. . . . We admire his superhuman efforts, but we do not hear him utter one word about humanity." —Venturi

does not mean simply to reproduce contours . . . drawing is also expression, the inner form, the plane, modelling"—was, as we shall see, almost exactly that of Matisse a century later, and Ingres' draftsmanship anticipated the Picasso of the classical nymphs and linear portraits.

Ingres began his career, oddly enough, with a determination to break away from David's formal prison by emulating the primitives. "The formless beginnings of certain arts," he wrote, "sometimes contain, fundamentally, more perfection than the perfected art." But very soon he fell into line, criticized his pupils for studying in Florence rather than Rome, became the idol of Théophile Gautier and his cult of art for art's sake, and ended up by making the academic pronouncement that "there is nothing essential to be found in art after Phidias and Raphael." By 1846 the French critic Thoré was able to call Ingres "the most romantic artist of the Nineteenth Century, if romanticism be an exclusive love of form, an absolute indifference to all the mysteries of human life, scepticism in philosophy and politics, selfish detachment from all common and socially unifying sentiments. The doctrine of art for art's sake is, in effect, a kind of materialistic brahminism which absorbs its adepts, not indeed in the contemplation of things eternal, but in the monomania of external and perishable form." [4]

Ingres and Delacroix were considered (and considered themselves) the two mutually hostile poles of painting in their time; so much so, that when they met accidentally at a ball and shook hands it was considered a triumph of *esprit de corps.* How different, actually, was the aesthetic philosophy of these two artists whose pictures, for all their divergent stress on line and color, are alike in seeking ideals outside reality? If Delacroix's best-known work, the "Scenes from the Massacre at Scio," be compared with Ingres' celebrated "Bain Turc" it will be seen at once how extraordinarily *dated* both pictures are. There is nothing dated about a Giotto because reality—the artist's emotional involvement in his world—is timeless. But for all its incomparable draftsmanship "Bain Turc" remains what it always was: a pornographic fantasy. It is vulgar not because of its subject but for the literary dimensions of its vision and the febrile quality of its sensuality. Similarly, the "Massacre" does not make us participate in war or identify ourselves with its victims because the romantic formalist is so conscious of the poses of his figures and the picturesqueness of their setting that we have to shake ourselves to remember that we are not shopping for curios in a gypsy bazaar.

Delacroix, though he travelled in North Africa and generally chose subjects of an exotic nature for his important pictures, repudiated Romanticism. From his *Journal* [5] one gets the impression that he was far more obsessed with recapturing the "objectivity" of the Greeks and the Romans than was Ingres. There also he makes the extraordinary but typically French observation that what elevates LaFontaine above Shakespeare or Michelangelo is "taste." He considers Watteau and even Rubens "too artistic" and places Ruisdael's landscapes "at the summit of art" above Rembrandt "because the art in them is completely hidden from view."

But while Delacroix with his conscious mind was a classicist who helped almost as much as Ingres to prepare the way for formalism in our time, there was a contradictory instinct in him that makes many of his unpremeditated drawings and some of his grandiloquent paintings the harbingers of expressionism as well. Noticing that a picture by Delacroix was even more effective from a distance than close up, Baudelaire concluded that "it inspires none the less feelings of sumptuousness, of joy or melancholy . . . as if the color *thinks for itself* independently of the objects it envelopes." Delacroix had developed this expressive use of pigments from a close study of Constable's "Hay Wain" which was exhibited in Paris in 1824. His appropriation of the English landscapist's revolutionary "division" of pure colors applied in short strokes, and of the glittering highlights that accompanied this procedure, gave Delacroix's pictures, technically

■

[4] *Le Salon de 1846,* by T. Thoré, Paris, 1846.
[5] *The Journal of Eugène Delacroix,* translated from the French by Walter Pach, 1937.

speaking, a place in the direct ancestry of Impressionism and Pointillism—a place to which they were entitled also by reason of that deliberate lack of involvement in his subjects I have already mentioned. But this method of applying paint did not give Delacroix an outlet for the instinctive passion he was at such pains to suppress. (In an unguarded moment he admitted "I thrive on the upsurge of my own feelings.") It did, however, permit him to endow what would otherwise have been scenes of mere literary or historical content with an indefinable aura of personal emotion. It is this quality, perhaps, that accounts for the otherwise surprising admiration for Delacroix expressed by such an essentially religious painter as Van Gogh.

Delacroix's "Scenes from the Massacre of Scio." Superficially the antithesis of Ingres' linear formalism, actually its complement in terms of action. Overloaded "content" with a minimum of expressive human or spiritual values.

Realism: Millet, Corot, Courbet

I touch but briefly on three giants of the next generation because their work is distinguished neither by this rage of the spirit nor by its contrary, the consuming will to externalize form. Is Courbet a photographic realist? Is Corot a minor nature poet? Is Millet a sentimental propagandist of Rousseau's Noble Savage (Marx's Heroic Worker)? Obviously all three were much more.

Millet's limitation was in placing so much stress on the discovery of the timelessness of human activity and the basic forms he revived for this characterization that he tended to reduce man to a series of posters: Patience, Endurance, Weariness, and the like. Millet's academic drafts-manship may, as Venturi suggests, be attributable to his having taken a course opposite to that of Daumier who set out from politics and attained to art: Millet "sets out from the academy and reaches a social and religious rhetoric—incidentally, a far from contemptible one." [6]

Courbet's "Woman with a Parrot." The stage of realistic formalism immediately preceding the enthronement of the Academy in the painting of Bouguereau and the sculpture of Forest Lawn. Venturi rightly calls this picture a "staggering blunder" and "an essay in cold-blooded eroticism."

Corot, in his early work a tonal realist, and a prophet of Formalism by reason of his balancing of volumes and light, became so absorbed in his late landscapes by memory and by the diffusion of light (he was the first to apply the word "impression" to painting) that he lost sight not only of content but of form itself. Corot was a gentle soul who loved to walk in the country and contemplate nature in terms of its values as the raw material of painting. It was his genius to give life if not exactly per-sonality to inanimate objects; but in the process he tended to treat the

■

[6] "Daumier" by Lionello Venturi, in *Modern Painters,* 1947.

human physiognomy as landscape and man himself as a diminutive inter-
loper in a sylvan world.

Courbet, much the strongest of the three, was as much bemused by
structural appearance as Corot had been by effects of light. The invention
of photography, with its groupings caught by the shutter in "accidental"
poses, and its blurred focus, seems to have affected both artists in these
differing respects. But Courbet's healthier emphasis on the captured slice
of life, on *content*, was a reflection of his superior capacity for experience.
An artist, he said, ought to be not only a painter but also a man; only a
man could create a living art.

Daumier's "Rue Transnonain, 15 April 1834." In this early lithograph Daumier picks up expressive content at the point where Goya left it, at the same time contributing an indictment of
the squalid waste and heartlessness of the times that would be as valid one hundred years later
as the day it was drawn.

The art that Courbet created was living, full of personalities—especially his own, for he was in love with his own appearance and infatuated
by his life as an artist as well as his art. That art shocked his contemporaries for it seemed that Courbet was giving to common types and even
to the trivial encounter an undeserved dignity. But Courbet did not stop
with that. He tried to encompass social revolution in his painting. He
assayed the grand manner of such masters as Titian, Hals and Raphael.
For the first venture he lacked understanding, and for the second taste.
Within the narrow frame of reference of his personal life Courbet created
an art that is still moving, but for an art of expressive content his lack of

Daumier's "Don Quixote and Sancho Panza." Painted thirty or forty years after the lithograph, this painting is to the former what Goya's "Executions" is to his print from *The Disasters of War*—a universally comprehensible expression of mankind's tragic predicament.

imagination and his materialistic distrust of ideas, religion, romance and mystery were too great a handicap.

Daumier's Heart

If Cézanne is the most over-esteemed of the great painters of the Nineteenth Century, Daumier is surely the most neglected. For all his earthy realism, Courbet with his dictum that a painter "ought to paint only what his eyes can see" anticipated not only Cézanne's formalism but Matisse's. Daumier was bound by no such tyranny to nature. The essential difference between Courbet and Daumier is in the story of their meeting one day after both men had refused Louis-Philippe's Legion of Honor.

"Great man!" Courbet is said to have shouted. "Like me you have rejected their dirty decoration! But why so quietly? One should do things of this kind with noise and show!"

"No, no, Courbet," Daumier replied, shaking his head reproachfully, "I did what I thought right. I am satisfied. But the whole matter is no business of the public's."

This absence of sham, of doing anything for effect, is as much the heart of Daumier's painting as it is of the man. And it is as much a characteristic of the two great painters between whom Daumier stands in succession of spiritual penetration—Rembrandt and Van Gogh. The lives of Titian or Vermeer or Matisse offer no clues to their art because their art is self-contained. Daumier's life *is* his art. Beginning in the Paris that saw

Goya's last lithographs, it unfolds during the eighteen years (1830-48) when the young artist produced four thousand engravings and stones for *La Caricature* and *Le Charivari,* went to jail for pillorying the monumental dishonesty of the King, and turned from political to social satire in disillusionment with the barbaric excesses of the revolutionists of '48. Slowly Daumier's life begins to yield its by-product of painting—that quintessential statement of the humanity "documented" in the four thousand prints. Encouraged by no public yet unembittered by the lack of one, he now sums up a lifetime of sympathetic observation in a symbolism as timeless as the late Beethoven quartets yet as poignantly of its age as Balzac's novels. It is noteworthy that Daumier's one recorded epigram is "Il faut être de son temps." It is pleasant to recall, too, that Balzac himself testified to his friend's stature when he remarked that Daumier "has Michelangelo's blood in his veins."

Baudelaire, who was not familiar with Daumier's oils but as usual went to the heart of the matter, wrote: "Daumier knows all the absurd misery, all the folly, all the pride of the small bourgeois—this type at once commonplace and eccentric—for he has lived intimately with them and loves them." The emphasis is on love. Daumier hated impersonal government but that was as far as his hatred went. Like Orozco after him, he does not hesitate to poke fun at those professing the same cause as his own. Among artists, members of a profession not noted for its tolerance, Daumier is the greatest democrat. What moved him to heights of indignation was not that governments could oppress but that citizens could abdicate their dignity as human beings by becoming pawns and puppets. "He was a republican spontaneously," another contemporary remarked. "It was the air he breathed. He was of the people and he loved them from the bottom of his heart." People who visited the Isle St.-Louis fifty years after the artist's death could look out of his studio widow with astonishment that the scene in the street below should be "pure Daumier." Arrogance was another artist's trait totally lacking in Daumier. Gripping the arm of a friend with whom he once was walking through the streets, he said "We at least have art to comfort us, but what have these wretched folk got?" The Goncourts met him one evening when he was a little drunk and quote him as saying "How orderly I must be getting! In the old days I knocked my head against the stars, but now I can't even climb a lamppost!"

The old artist may have been alluding to the activity of his life as a cartoonist when he was jailed three times for expressing subversive sentiments and on the basis of that experience penned his tremendous indictments of legal hypocrisy. Now it was different: his cartoons were no longer in demand, and on the few occasions when they were commissioned, he found himself accepting with the bitter knowledge that this, his only means of livelihood, was taking precious time from the painting nobody wanted. Then again, he may have been commenting ironically on an aspect of his art that was already attracting unfavorable attention—a reverence for human suffering that went so far as to sympathize with vain ambition and condone stupidity. Why else should he have painted Don

Quixote and Sancho Panza over and over again in those last few years?

These Spanish characters, the unstable knightly idealist and his stolid but good-natured attendant, came to serve Daumier, the professed atheist, as the dominant symbols in an art more truly religious than any since Rembrandt's.

On the few occasions when Daumier did paint overtly Christian subjects—"The Good Samaritan" and "Ecce Homo"—his treatment of them was more than adequate. The first was a commission on which his patron reneged as soon as the finished picture was presented. In the second, Daumier caught unmistakably that aspect of Christ's terrible isolation in the face of popular insensitivity which has preoccupied every modern interpreter of the Passion from Ensor and Obin to Beckmann and Lebrun. It may be assumed that the reason Daumier did not more often paint Christian subjects was a sense of the gulf that yawned between Christ's teachings and his observations of the lip-service the clergy paid to them. But in his profoundly spiritual art Daumier is not at all like the sensual Rabelais to whom he has sometimes been compared, nor like Hogarth whose realistic indictment appeals only to the brain.

Delacroix, like Balzac, sensed Daumier's affinity to Michelangelo, and there is certainly something of the Pauline frescoes in the low-keyed color and brooding memory of the French artist's last pictures. But it is a Michelangelo with compassion, never setting himself above the victims of the injustice he portrays, and without despair. Daumier's world, someone has said, is stripped of its façade but left all its human values. He regards man's life as essentially a gallant attitude. "Honest atheist that he was," writes his biographer, "Daumier was nearer than he thought, in his purity of heart, to those who know that the Kingdom of God is not of this world, but for whom this knowledge is the best of all reasons for keeping the Kingdom of God in their hearts." [7]

The result, in terms of painting, is an art of transfigured symbols and universal content. It is as accessible to the common man as it is to the intellectual because the experiences it depicts are those of a particular human being in a particular place. Yet it is pure painting in a sense having nothing to do with aesthetic detachment, the quintessence of such sanity and deep engagement with life that nothing in the end is anecdotal, timely, or exactly definable, the whole canvas being charged with its creator's incandescent spirit. "It was he," said Théodore de Banville, "who first drew nature and material objects out of their anonymity, obliging them to take part in the Human Comedy, where sometimes trees share in the absurdity of their proprietor, or, in the midst of a domestic scene, the vases on the table start snarling with ironic rage."

As far as contributing to the dominant Nineteenth Century preoccupations with light, color, form, as ends in themselves, is concerned, Daumier was hopelessly off the track. Even those contemporaries who admired his plates showed no interest in his paintings, and he was followed by no school. This same neglect was to be the fate of the next giant of expressive

---

[7] *Daumier* by Jacques Lassaigne, Paris, 1938.

content, Vincent Van Gogh, as it would be to a somewhat lesser degree of Georges Rouault in our time. But in order to understand the causes of Van Gogh's isolation it will be necessary to return to the mainstream of painting.

Manet's "Déjeuner sur l'Herbe." Obverse of Daumier's humane expressionism, this deliberately artificial pastorale returns to the mainstream of Nineteenth Century formalism, setting the stage for the still more abstract charades of Seurat, Cézanne and Matisse.

Manet and the Impressionists

In 1863, sixteen years before Daumier's death, Édouard Manet's "Déjeuner sur l'Herbe" was blackballed from the official Salon in Paris and became the feature attraction in the first Salon des Refusés. In 1874, five years before Daumier's death, the first Impressionist Exhibit was held, including the work of two painters, Claude Monet and Camille Pissaro, who had just returned from London where they had studied Constable's technique. In this same exhibit hung "The House of the Hanged Man at Auvers," the first characteristic painting by Paul Cézanne. And ten years later, only five years after Daumier's death, Seurat began painting his pointillist masterpiece, "La Grande Jatte," now in the Chicago Art Institute. These are the key dates of the unfolding of modern art in the eyes of its historians.

Seurat's "Sunday Afternoon on the Island of Grande Jatte." Not since the mysteriously static statements of Piero della Francesca has a moment in time and place been frozen into monumental immobility with such success as in this formalist masterpiece.

Manet's picture, after the lapse of nearly a century, naturally seems the least revolutionary. And actually the scandal it caused at the Salon came about less because of its technique than because the male members of the picnic it portrayed happened to be fully clothed while the women were nude—though Manet's friends were quick to point out that Giorgione's precisely similar convention in the "Fête Champêtre" at the nearby Louvre was causing no raised eyebrows. What probably stimulated the blood pressure of the philistines was that the scene was so obviously contemporary and that the indifferent males were so clearly portraits of Manet's friends. This in itself was a clue to what was really radical in the picture. Form, not sex, love or picnicking, was its subject.

Manet's career seems to have taken off from the point where Couture, his master, had remarked sarcastically of his pupil's efforts "You will never be more than the Daumier of your time." Resolved to escape a fate so degrading, Manet began by painting figures in flat patterns somewhat in the manner of the Japanese prints then entering Europe for the first time. When Courbet accused him of making pictures that looked like playing cards, he was not insulted at all. He had already determined to do away with expressive content; the content would be the picture itself. In the "Déjeuner sur l'Herbe," and in the even more shocking (to his contemporaries) "Olympia," the unidealized nude that immediately followed it, Manet dispensed with Corot's adjusted values, laying the paint on directly with the edges of the brushstrokes clearly indicated. This was the same method we have already seen Goya experimenting with in his "Maja Nude." Manet carried it much further. In "Olympia," Robb points out, Manet painted a nude who is no longer a woman, and he would have subscribed wholeheartedly to Whistler's pronouncement that "Art should stand alone and appeal to the artistic sense of eye and ear, without confounding this with emotions entirely foreign to it, as devotion, pity, love, patriotism and the like."

The Impressionists, in their effort to capture the purely visual moment, tended to waive not only expressive content but subject-matter itself. Thus they carried Manet's aestheticism a step further. But in so far as Monet and Pisarro were naturalists, fascinated as Velasquez had been by advances in optics (in their case by the extent to which such scientists as Helmholz and Maxwell had shown that light was a physical phenomenon), the Impressionists quickly fell into a dreary academicism of their own. Monet painted the façade of Rouen Cathedral no fewer than forty times in order merely to record the changes that took place in its visual aspect from dawn to dusk. It was in revolt against their tendency to make the picture no more than an amorphous shimmer of color that Cézanne and Seurat now began to re-emphasize structure.

Structure, of course, can be just as much an abstraction as reflected light. In fact, it quickly came to be. But for the time being, it played a creative role in rescuing painting from the shapelessness to which the Impressionists had carried it. In ways that were to prove less influential, such untypical Impressionists as Renoir and Degas had already rebelled against this impassivity. Renoir revitalized the sensuality of Boucher and the Venetians through his application of atmospherically generalized color to the human body. Degas had emphasized arrested movement in the startling angles then for the first time being revealed by still-photography. The points of departure of Seurat and Cézanne seemed at the time less daring.

Seurat, who died young and painted a very few pictures, was an artist with a relentlessly analytical mind. The logic of Impressionism in his hand quickly reduced the divided brush-strokes of Monet and Pissaro into orderly dots of equal size. These he applied painstakingly and with extraordinary subtlety, juxtaposing pure and secondary hues, to form an over-all pattern through which and out of which his figures stand or glide like dancers in a classic ballet. Technically, Seurat was the culminating painter of Impressionism, but his passion for geometry, reminiscent of Piero della Francesca in its creation of an eternally "frozen" world, he shared with Cézanne.

Cézanne: The Architecture of Space

As the climactic figure in the Nineteenth Century drive for an abstract union of line, light, color and volume, and the father of Twentieth Century Formalism, Paul Cézanne's enormous shadow projects in so many directions as to defy analysis. To understand why genius of the magnitude of Cézanne's concerned itself unremittingly with problems having so little to do with life, we must remind ourselves that the intellectual atmosphere in France at the end of the Nineteenth Century was distinctly hostile to psychology, humanism and religion. Villier de l'Isle Adam's Axel, preferring perfect illusion to imperfect reality, had already made his famous announcement that life was something his servants could take care of for him. Huysman's Des Esseintes had refused to go on a journey

Cézanne's "Bathers." Climax of Nineteenth Century formalism, springboard to Twentieth Century Cubism and Non-objectivism. The triumph of this particular picture is in its successful distortion of earth, air, tree and flesh into a poetic unity of shapes in space defined by light.

lest he be disappointed with reality. Mallarmé was about to write that "A beautiful line without meaning is more beautiful than a less beautiful one with meaning." Flaubert considered writing a book without any subject at all. And Rimbaud, in Hauser's words, had "established deformity and grimace as means of expression, based in essentials on the feeling that the normal, spontaneous, spiritual attitudes are artistically sterile and that the poet must overcome the natural man within himself in order to discover the hidden meaning of things." Yet it was an age when painting, an urban art now brought together by opposition to the public, had come to dominate all the arts. "What a happy profession that of the painter is," the Goncourts could exclaim, "compared with that of the writer!" It was much easier to paint abstractions than to write them. Balzac's prophecy that the artist who estranges himself from life will end by destroying art fell on deaf ears.

All this was Cézanne's heritage. As a close friend of Zola, his provincial life could hardly have immured him against it. He inherited too—in reaction against the "soft" aestheticism of the Impressionists—a strong conviction of the primacy of the intellect. His early work, influenced by Courbet, was realistic. But it showed already a fondness for structural composition and for those massive forms he was later to call "the bones of nature." The contradictory elements in Cézanne's style then begin to appear. His passion for uncovering an abstract geometrical pattern at the roots of the visible world is opposed to a sense of mission in carrying the scientific naturalism of the Impressionists to a logical conclusion, not with dots as Seurat had, but by means of planes subtly overlaid to bring out the form behind the visual sensation. This was the Cézanne who threatened out of nature and with the tools of the Impressionists to create an art fit once more "for the museums." The other Cézanne—eventually the two became one—was the theorist who carried out his promise to "revive Poussin upon the face of Nature." How he painted still-life after still-life, cunningly distorting the shapes to emphasize the rotundity of an apple, the verticality of a vase; how he analyzed Mont St.-Victoire until nothing remained but its impressive mass; and how he left a programme for the generation that was to follow him in his famous admonition to look in nature for the sphere, the cone and the cylinder—are too well known to recapitulate at length here.

Cézanne's great accomplishments are also too familiar to rehearse—if this were the place for it. Those who ask of art no more than that it rearrange the scenery of outdoors and indoors in planes of singing color monumentally disposed, are satisfied that no artist offers more. We are concerned here with a contemporary of Cézanne who occupies a less exalted place in current fashion and who tried desperately in his tragic life to say less than he felt—under the inescapable sanction of Cézanne's formal mystique.

The Tragedy of Van Gogh

So instinctively was Van Gogh the artist of expressive content that he seems not to have painted or even drawn with a pencil until forced to it by the realization that he had no other means of changing the world. It was enough for him in the beginning to follow his father's calling, to be a preacher: how better serve humanity? How better communicate one's love of mankind? But Van Gogh's father, though a good man, would probably not have recognized Christ had He re-appeared in Amsterdam. He was alarmed by the unconventional religious behavior of his son. What was this business of going to the poets for evidence of God's love—poets famed for their immorality like Baudelaire and Heine? And this strange comparison of Christ with the Christ of Rembrandt and Duerer?

At La Borinage, where Vincent went among the miners to serve his novitiate, he made a bad impression among the hierarchy from the outset. He took his duties as seriously as the workers were taking their work. He became one of the community, dressing as poorly as the poorest, giving away his clothes, his money, even his bed. No wonder the Church put a quick end to this career of Van Gogh's! And no wonder Meier-Graefe at the beginning of his biography of the painter [8] stresses the point that this man "who drew like a child" had none of the self-conscious, playful, inventive qualities that the type artist has, or is supposed to have. "But if," he then decided, "the word artist denotes supreme self-sacrifice and the ability to give oneself up unreservedly for the world and for the service

Van Gogh's "Potato Eaters." A "primitive" (but not primitivistic) tribute to the expressive art of Hals and Rembrandt. The masterpiece of Van Gogh's pre-French period before reigning formalism censored his chosen content, causing it to re-appear in more sophisticated and tormented guises.

of humanity; if it is a synonym for a man of such moral tenor that he only sets a further goal to his aspiration as his consciousness gains in the deepening perception of Nature and her laws, then Vincent was an artist and the greatest of our time."

When Vincent was rejected by the Church and decided to make art

■

[8] *Vincent Van Gogh: A Biographical Study* by Julius Meier-Graefe, London, 1951.

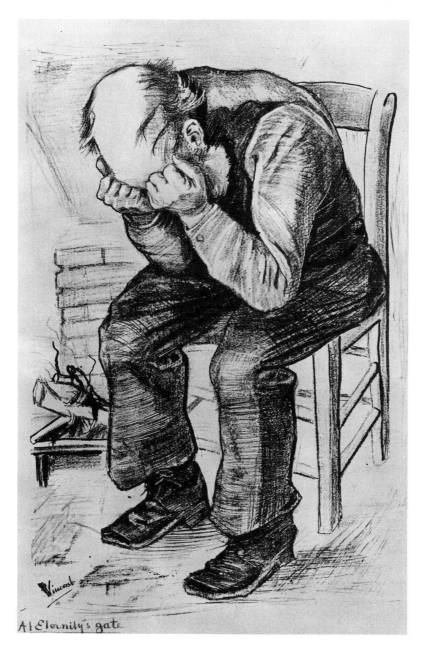

Van Gogh's "At Eternity's Gate" (lithograph). A rare example of the painter's mature art in which emotion stems from the subject itself rather than being manifested indirectly through technique.

the means by which he would communicate his love of man, he rationalized the shift to himself in this way: "If a man loves Rembrandt profoundly, then in his heart of hearts he knows God." Naturally enough, Vincent's approach to painting was like his approach to the Church. It was the approach of a primitive, of an innocent man. He wanted more than anything to paint a worker, the simplest of men, and accurately, from the man's expression to the last nail in his shoes. He wanted his work to be popular. One whose heart is full of love, a love without ulterior motives, has no secrets. He thought of drawing a series of "Heads of the People."

Van Gogh's "Night Café." Essentially religious criticism of contemporary life conveyed through devices of developing Expressionism—violent orange of swinging lamps, sulphurous olive greens and yellows of tilted table and floor—as well as in the sordidness of the scene itself.

They would be in lithograph since that was the cheapest medium and would sell for ten cents. His early pictures are in sombre colors and deep shadow, reflecting his scorn for the Impressionists: Old Dutch vs. Fashionable Paris. The hands of the "Potato Eaters" (1885) are modelled on the hands of the "Lady Regents" in Hals' great picture. The "Peasant's Head" of the same year has the features of Hals but the mouth and eyes of Rembrandt's "Margaret Trip." His "Peasant with a Broom" suggests Millet, a painter for whom Van Gogh already had great respect, but is without any of Millet's lyric sentiment. His "Still Life with Bottles" might have been painted by A. P. Ryder, the American recluse whose expressionist art so resembles that of both the early Van Gogh and Daumier.

So much for the Dutch Van Gogh, his life, his artistic ancestors and descendants, his smoky pictures. The scene now shifts to Paris. The year is 1886. Van Gogh has only four more years to live and has not yet created a single one of the pictures by which the world knows him. All those paintings are the result of a tension between Holland and France, innocence and sophistication, expressive content and purely aesthetic values, the art of religion and the religion of art. It was a tension that was to end with the artist's self-mutilation and suicide. Whether Van Gogh would have become a better painter had he remained at home is as futile to conjecture as whether he would have retained his sanity and lived to a ripe old age. "I do not need to go out of my way to express sadness and extreme loneliness," he was soon to complain from his self-imposed exile; "I have risked my life for my work; for it, I have lost my reason."

All that one can say is that the conflict between these two worlds enveloped Van Gogh immediately. First his impressionable nature was overwhelmed by what the Impressionists, when he actually saw their pictures, were doing with pure colors. Pisarro and his doctrinaire circle regarded all painting not done from nature as "literary." Meier-Graefe says that Van Gogh followed their practice "as if it were one of the Ten Commandments." He met Seurat and was bowled over by that ascetic artist's devotion to art and the will-power with which he made scientific procedures the handmaidens of his classic vision. The theories behind all this meticulous labor were not only incomprehensible to Van Gogh; they were something against which everything in his nature must have rebelled. But he painted pointillist pictures like a demon. His brother compared these canvases to those of a man who tries to speak without words. When he met Lautrec and Gauguin, Van Gogh knew that their flat patterns and the Japanese prints they derived them from were elements that he must assimilate. Seeing his first Cézanne he was told as if by an angel of Judgment that he would be damned unless he went to Provence.

He arrived in Arles in February of 1888. He slunk about, Meier-Graefe says, "like a Protestant in a Cathedral during High Mass. What had he, from the North, to do with this riot of color? . . . He began to paint. What else could he do? . . . Ten pictures of the flowery gardens of Arles in as many days." The great paintings of those final two years of Van Gogh's life are the tragic witnesses of the heroism with which the artist forced nature and inanimate objects—houses, bridges, cobblestones, bottles, bedrooms—to express his religious vision. His frustration at the self-deprivation of significant subject-matter is apparent when we consider two facts. First, he expresses over and over again during those years, and in a variety of ways, his envy of those artists who obeyed no such censor. He became obsessed by Delacroix and Courbet, visiting the local museums to stand in awe before their canvases. But Delacroix's "cosmic forging of past into present" was as impossible for him to capture as Courbet's realism, limited to the projection of a grandiose personality. The familiar images of the less sophisticated Millet he repainted, endowing them with such tragic depth as he would have lavished on content of his own choosing—had he felt capable of such choice. In the few instances where, perhaps with the aged Rembrandt's example to fortify him, he did choose his proper subjects—the self-portraits, the poolroom, and finally the asylum with its inmates—he painted his greatest pictures.

The terrible crisis of December 23rd was touched off by an argument between Van Gogh and Gauguin that reveals clearly enough the Dutch artist's state of mind. Gauguin complained that Van Gogh really admired only Daumier and Rembrandt and actually detested Ingres, Raphael and Degas. Van Gogh's presentation of his own ear "as a souvenir of myself" followed. If he could not make Gauguin understand the meaning of reality in art, perhaps he would recognize it in the flesh!

The reality that Gauguin was after is characterized by nothing more strikingly than the "Yellow Christ" which he painted at Pont Aven in Brittany before coming to Arles and which Van Gogh saw through immediately. It is beautifully painted and composed. It is picturesquely romantic in the nostalgia it evokes for the "touching" devotion of simple folk. It is pseudo-primitive. And it is as phony as Dali's "Virgin of the Atomic Age." The reality that Van Gogh sought after and that he briefly captured in the confines of St.-Rémy was the reality of modern man trapped in the madhouse of his egoism, his materialism and his incapacity for selfless love. The St.-Rémy asylum had been, ironically, a cloister, and its nurses were nuns. "Just as someone had turned this cloister into a lunatic asylum filled with so-called sisters of mercy [Meier-Graefe reconstructs Van Gogh's thoughts], so the pastors had turned the teachings of Christ into a sin-

ister legacy. . . . He [Van Gogh] had a loathing for these sisters with their starched religion, who saw in their patients not invalids but men possessed of devils. He would have liked to send them to learn a little decent feeling from the inhabitants of the House of Madame Chose."

This precise mission was to be undertaken within thirteen years by an artist who was himself a devout Catholic, thereby fulfilling the destiny of Daumier as well as Van Gogh, and carrying the torch for an art of expressive content into the formal gardens of the Twentieth Century.

Gauguin's "Yellow Christ."

PART TWO [C]

The Religion of Experience *vs.*
The Religion of Form:

The Twentieth Century

Rouault's "Red Haired Woman." Expressive content reasserting itself on the threshold of the Twentieth Century in this angry but plastically masterful protest against the degradation of the human spirit.

PART TWO [C]

The Religion of Experience vs.
The Religion of Form:

The Twentieth Century

If expressive content failed to be the primary consideration in the art of the Nineteenth Century, one may still assert that through the achievements of Goya, Daumier and Van Gogh it held its own. In the art of the first half of the Twentieth Century this is no longer so. Picasso and Matisse are by far the dominating figures in these fifty years. Both of them make guarded use of expressive elements in their work, but its main preoccupation is formal, as I shall endeavor to show when discussing their painting in the later sections of this chapter. Presently I am going to trace the divergent paths followed by those contemporary artists who for various reasons declined to travel the Formalist highway. Some, perhaps all, paid the price of being out of step—an isolation from the principal theatre leading to a sense of strain, sometimes of eccentricity in even the strongest spirits; to an embittered self-pity and often philistinism in the weaker ones. Some, no doubt, went astray for want of good eyesight. But the survivors were tough, in the best sense—they had to be. If their art does not constitute (as I hope and believe) a prophecy of things to come, it will surely be regarded by future generations as the most accurate, deeply felt and moving record of our epoch.

Lest I be accused of over-simplification, this is the place to reiterate that *form* is a principal component of all art and that every true artist seeks to make the forms in his own pictures simple as well as expressive. Van Gogh, as we have seen, could not fail to be impressed by the formal innovations of Seurat and Cézanne. For like reasons, the sensitive expressive artist of today, if he has not been directly influenced by those masters, will hardly escape, even if he would like to, the revolutionary discoveries of their two principal heirs.

The Reassertion of Spirit: Rouault

Rouault, the first and perhaps the greatest expressive artist of our time, is no exception to this rule. For though his mature art seems to be the negation of the pure, the formal, the abstract, and in its isolated spirituality as much a law unto itself as Daumier's, it has its roots in the post-Impressionist revolt against formlessness, and in its final phase aspires to a rigidity as stylized as a Byzantine enamel and as untormented as a Matisse.

Like Matisse, Rouault began his career as a pupil of the liberal academician Gustave Moreau, and like Matisse he exhibited with the so-called "wild beasts" (*fauves*) of formalistic expressionism in the Salon of 1905. But there the identification stops. Rouault, who was Moreau's star pupil and whose style (unlike Matisse's) owed a great deal to his master, was already devoutly religious.[1]

Moreau had urged Rouault not to go into religious retirement. "You are young," Rouault quotes him as saying, "in spite of your precocious experience of life. *You must live* and learn to live in your own way, not according to bookish theories . . ." The young artist took this advice to heart and went back to his childhood experiences rather than to fashionable modes of painting for his inspiration. He had been born under the exploding shells of 1871. He grew up with a grandfather who admired Rembrandt and Courbet and collected Daumier lithographs. "As a child face to face with reality," he says, "I went first to the school of Daumier before knowing Raphael." At fourteen he was apprenticed to a stained-glass craftsman. In 1903 he read Léon Bloy's *La Femme Pauvre*, with the result that he stopped painting merely religious subjects and started painting pictures out of an inner religious compulsion. Bloy, a passionate convert to Catholicism, had written that "if art does not go on its knees . . . it must necessarily go on its belly." He had concluded his novel with the words: "There is only one grief—not to be a saint." Moreau, who had confirmed Rouault's passion for Rembrandt, had also warned his pupil that the spiritual art of the Middle Ages grew out of more than a preoccupation with the "real" and that "art is a furious tracking down of the inner feelings solely by means of plastic expression."

Bloy, oddly enough, was shocked by Rouault's first characteristic pictures. The Catholic writer had himself been converted by prostitutes, but he seems to have been no better prepared for Rouault's daemonic women of the streets than Van Gogh's theological advisers had been for the Dutch artist's uncompromising realism. Bloy reprimanded Rouault for being "exclusively interested in the ugly," but as Soby points out, Rouault's very choice of prostitutes as his symbols of earthly degradation followed his reading of Bloy, and far from reflecting an "interest in the ugly" they reflected Bloy's similar "frenzied preoccupation with sin and redemption."

Rouault himself has explained the direction of his work, denying at

■

[1] James Thrall Soby, whose Museum of Modern Art monograph on Rouault is my principal source for this account of Rouault's development, tells us that Moreau regarded religion as mainly an iconographical storehouse. But even in Rouault's earliest work Soby sees "if inconclusively, the direction in which he was going, *a direction in which it might be necessary to forego aesthetics, in a measure, in order to remember Faith.*" (My italics.)

the same time charges of undue influence from the worldly Degas and the cynical Lautrec. "I underwent then," he says, "a moral crisis of the most violent sort. I experienced things which cannot be expressed by words and I began to paint with an outrageous lyricism which disconcerted everybody. . . . It was not the influence of Lautrec, Degas or the moderns that inspired me, but an inner necessity and perhaps the unconscious desire not to fall full-length into conventional religious subject matter." Hello, another Catholic writer who influenced Rouault in this formative period, had described art's function as telling the truth—the religious truth: "Art has said that evil was beautiful. Art must be one of the forces which will cure the imagination; it must say that evil is ugly." But the public was no more receptive to Rouault's tragic vision of life than Bloy had been—the public was just becoming adjusted to the shimmering water-lilies of Monet. Nor were Rouault's fellow-artists impressed; most of them then preferred decorative to psychological expressionism. Nor was the Church: the Church would wait almost fifty years to welcome this artist who painted the life of the spirit with a fervor not seen since the days of El Greco.

It may have been this triple neglect which accounts for the preoccupation with technique that increases noticeably as Rouault ages. Briefly in 1907, under the spell of Cézanne ("That seer of painting," Rouault had called him) the prostitutes and disreputable clowns had turned into odalisques and bathers. In 1908, however, Rouault returned to the mood of savage indignation and painted his most unforgettable harlot, "The Red-haired Woman," and that series of near-sighted, prosperous, Daumier-like judges which culminates in the cross-eyed "Mr. X" of 1911. Of this climactic image of bourgeois materialism Rouault later wrote: "It is to forget Mr. X, who kept haunting my brain although I had not yet created him pictorially, that from 1897 on I painted Crucifixions, Flagellations, occasionally some pathetic clowns, prostitutes, certain types of living dead-wood and various different landscapes. In painting this sort of thing—not to stir up malice or to incite class against class—I had no spiteful intentions, no particular grudge. But what do I honestly know about it, and *who* knows himself?" James Johnson Sweeney calls one of the "Three Judges" in 1913 the complete antithesis of classicism—"an urgent eccentric vitality, a brilliant vigor, a hard intense abstraction and Celtic unfriend-liness—a contemporary parallel of that terrifying formal distortion whereby primitive man knew how to create a vision of the super-real."

It is possible that Sweeney would never have used the words "formal" and "abstraction" if he had been unfamiliar with the pictures that were to follow. By 1916 the spirit of awful protest in the artist had burned itself out. His greatest pictures had been painted. Perhaps the mass horror of the War left Rouault with a feeling that the easel painting as a means of spiritual communication had become anachronistic.[2] Who was buying his pictures anyway? Not the masses. Not the Church. A few rich collectors were buying them—perhaps the wives of the very judges and Mr. X's

■

[2] See page 161.

he had been exposing. Two avenues of expression remained open to him. He could condense his social-spiritual message into engravings that might conceivably reach a wider audience. He could seek in his paintings to rise above the moment's images of evil and guilt, sublimating the violence of his feelings into timeless symbols—Resignation, Dignity, Love and the like—that could evoke a more universal response. Rouault acted upon both impulses.

Miserere et Guerre, the great series of etchings which Rouault executed between 1914 and 1927, bears much the same central relationship to his work as a whole as the "Caprices" and "Disasters of War" taken together bear to the work of Goya. It may be compared to the prints of

Rouault's "Mr. X." In daring to come so close to caricature (yet avoiding it) the artist in this emphatic composite portrait of the smug, juridical petty official creates a valid archetype.

Daumier, too, if the quantitative difference is discounted and if one bears in mind that Daumier was making his daily bread out of stones even before he had begun to paint, whereas Rouault was carrying over into his fifty-eight copper-plates all the purely "painterly" preoccupations he had once lavished on his canvases. This difference in approach is important in evaluating the significance of *Miserere et Guerre* and its fate. Rouault tells us that he began by making drawings in India ink, and from these, paintings. The drawings were transferred onto copper by mechanical means, following which Rouault endeavored by every conceivable means —aquatint, drypoint, roulette, and applications of acid with a brush—to recapture the rhythm of the original drawings and the darker intensities of the paintings; sometimes, he says, he made as many as fifteen successive states of a subject.

What Rouault was trying to convey in this series of engravings, so clearly inspired by the First World War's collective denial of Christianity, has been ably summed up by Monroe Wheeler in his introduction to the

Museum of Modern Art's edition of *Miserere et Guerre*. The message, Wheeler concludes, seems to be:

> Man's fate upon earth is tragic. It is very hard for him to be sincere, and he inclines to traduce and mask himself in his relationships, male to female, man to man. As a rule his hope is folly. Look at Plate 11, and read what is written there, " 'Tomorrow will be beautiful,' said the shipwrecked man as he sank into the sea." The everyday fate of man is to live by the sweat of his brow, never well enough. His love is in the subjunctive or in the future, never quite attainable. Whole nations are predestined to hunger and thirst and fear, to invasion, devastation, displacement. The future is myth and mystery; a vague reign of alien potentates, misrule of paranoiacs, dance of death.
>
> What shall man do? The great French artist feels that he is in the same plight as every man, Where can he turn? To the Church,

Rouault's "It is you, my Lord, I recognize you." Plate from the *Miserere et Guerre* (*Collection Museum of Modern Art*) showing the great religious painter's art at its purest and most compassionate. Subjectivity and refinement of means tend to limit audience to the devout and the sophisticated.

> the Evangels, Jesus Christ dead and buried, risen the third day.
>
> This is an epic without words; the story of an artist's implacable opposition to stupidity, his indignation at arrogance and brutishness, and his sympathy for fellow humanity. It is the *Comédie Humaine* of a great painter, the testimony of his own integrity maintained through solitude and sorrow.

From the point of view of our special inquiry, the question aroused by *Miserere et Guerre* is not simply how well it succeeds as a work of art, but why it failed in the artist's avowed intention of reaching a popular audience. "The least line or blur," Rouault had said, "can instruct us more than any number of indigestible pamphlets." The fact remains that only the most sophisticated of art lovers have warmed to the artist's religious message. It was not until 1948, twenty-four years after Rouault began them and eleven after their completion, that the plates were actually printed in France—and then in an edition of only 450 copies. Five years later a much larger edition of 5000 copies was issued by the Museum of Modern Art in New York. This was the most unkindest cut of all! For the Museum, Rouault was well aware, had long since become the focal point of Twentieth Century Formalism, that elaborate intellectualism which he had once scathingly described as "cerebral morphinomania" . . .

The reason, unquestionably, why Rouault's plates have not aroused much response except among art-lovers, is that Rouault himself is a product of French classicism and of the divorce between artist and public which enveloped its last (Formalist) phase. Only in his early period does he take the raw material of contemporary life, as Goya and Daumier did, and endow it through his expressive genius with universal meaning. In *Miserere et Guerre* he adapted traditional icons (Veronica's Veil, etc.) that had already lost their emotional meaning except to devout co-religionists. He created symbolic images of generalized vices such as Avarice, Indifference, Vanity, Sadism, and the like, and *related* these by means of suggestive references and obliquely ironic captions to the contemporary situation. The artistic vocabulary in which these symbolic pictures are couched is as remote from the life of Twentieth Century man as Rouault himself in the monastic isolation of his Paris *atelier* had become from the War, the Factory, the Tenement, the Prison, the Refugee Camp and the other manifestations of modern inhumanity he brooded over. However deeply he felt their impact, and the depth of that feeling is certainly in *Miserere et Guerre*, what he wished to communicate is not manifest to one whose taste has not already assimilated Byzantine mosaics, Gothic glass, Coptic tapestries, African sculpture and the linear shorthand of the Fauves.

According to Venturi, Rouault does not recall having begun a wholly new picture after 1916. He simply reworked old canvases thereafter. This would seem to indicate that the artist's vision became directed entirely *within;* indeed Rouault has said "We have only to work like the deaf and the mute; for painters I hardly dare say like the blind. Nevertheless it is sometimes good even for a painter to close his eyes for an instant." We are hardly surprised to learn that Rouault has left his "Crucifixion," begun during World War I, deliberately unfinished; in this case at least he seems to have sensed that reworking and polishing would destroy the original tragic content.

His last pictures have been cleansed of everything but the old man's interior vision. That vision is serene, but remote from life. "The Old King" (it is dated 1916-1936) has been overlaid with so much color that the subject and even much of the emotion that the artist must have once attached to it have been buried. Rouault's written tribute to the "unobtrusive Chardins" and to Poussin dates from this period. We admire these late Rouaults as we admire objects thrown up by the sea, so encrusted with barnacles, seaweed and salt that their original identity is indecipherable.

Rouault's "Old King." Black contours and jewel-rich impasto, heritage of the artist's early stained-glass apprenticeship, overload this late picture with a burden of paint more formal than expressive.

They exist for us as metamorphosis. Under the shimmer of impasto, expressive intensity has yielded to contemplative nirvana. With their decorative device of the painted frame within the picture, Rouault's very latest paintings approach, as Soby admits, "the ideal of art for its own sake which his figure pieces of 1905 and 1906 had so strenuously repudiated."

Soutine's Religion of Paint

A very different man and artist, but among moderns comparable only to Rouault in the degree to which he sometimes managed to invest paint itself with the drama of spiritual suffering, was Chaim Soutine. A distinction between the two men, however, is that Rouault, a devout Catholic, never pities himself or regards his personal trials as the basis for an indictment of the world. Soutine, lacking both self-control and the solace of faith in a higher Reality, tended to make every picture he painted, regardless of subject matter, the vehicle for expressing his exaltation, fury or frustration.

Soutine lived the whole of his life as an artist in and around Paris. It was the life of a bohemian and anarchist whose only religion was art. He was also a neurotic whose compulsion was to torment the wealthy patrons on whom he wholly depended for his livelihood. "Afraid of coming to be like other men, and losing his singularity as an artist," Soutine, in Monroe Wheeler's account of his truculent life,[3] oscillated between

■

[3] *Soutine,* by Monroe Wheeler, New York, Museum of Modern Art, 1950.

crises of his own making in a frenzy of forced effort. As a child in the
ghetto of Lithuania, he had been almost beaten to death by the son of a
rabbi who thought Soutine was making fun of his father by offering to
paint his portrait. In Paris the story is told of a poor woman who thought
she was owed money and whom Soutine refused to pay, burning up thou-
sand-franc notes before her eyes to emphasize his point. His painting,
with the turbulent landscapes and wildly slashing brushstrokes, may be
regarded as a kind of atonement for this pitilessness that accompanied his
anxiety, but more accurately it was his only way of making peace with
himself. Why he painted, Soutine could no more have explained than why

Soutine's "Maternity." With this artist, painting,
perhaps for the first time, is expressive regardless of content—and sometimes with no content
at all. Emotion in this picture, an exception in
Soutine's work, seems to stem from subject.

he endured life. His choice of subjects as time went on became "idle and
thoughtless," as Wheeler notes, but his conscience when it came to achieving a statement as loaded with emotion as he could make it never wavered.
He would go to fantastic lengths to achieve this end. When he painted
the hulking, fiery carcases of steer inspired by Rembrandt's awesome still-
life in the Louvre, he would hang sides of meat in his studio until decom-
position set in, paying someone to fan away the flies, drenching the rotten
flesh with buckets of fresh blood, and denouncing the neighbors who
complained of the smell as enemies of art. At one time he wielded his
brush with such violence that he dislocated his thumb. At other times he
would sink into moods of despair that made friends fear for his life. He
would write to one of them of ". . . this landscape that I cannot endure
. . . I am in Cagnes again against my will, where, instead of landscapes,
I shall be forced to do some miserable still-lifes. You will understand in
what a state of indecision I am. Can't you suggest some place for me?"

Then he would be back in Paris, starving himself before some strung-up chicken—in order to paint it *hungry;* or gaining entrance to a collector's home in order to slash one of his early pictures that now displeased him with his jackknife.

Soutine's idols were Rembrandt, Greco, Courbet, but in his own work he is a Rembrandt without compassion, a Greco without faith, a Courbet with no real *joie de vivre.* The Van Gogh of the writhing cypresses is there, but never the Van Gogh of Postmaster Roulin or the Hospital at Arles. Daumier's clouds are present but they do not twist and turn with sympathy over Daumier's humanity. The greatness—and the limitation— of Soutine is his ability to turn all this pessimism about life and exaltation before nature into a wild poetry. The intensest factor of his art may have been, as Wheeler says, "only *how* to express, not *what*—his ghastly anxiety lest the power and skill of his brush fail to fulfill the vision of his mind's eye." This was the next to last step that expressionism could take when reduced to nothing but the personal component. Only in such a late picture as the "Maternity" of 1942 do tradition and subject inadvertently combine to give Soutine's poetry, in Shakespeare's phrase, "a local habitation and a name."

Soutine's typical portraits and pastry-cooks, like his still-lifes and landscapes, are unrelated to anything but Soutine. Their coherence is the coherence of forms and color only. The final stage of this development in painting is the wholly abstract expressionism of the Dutch-American artist Willem de Kooning.[4] And it is not surprising that when de Kooning's more outgoing nature began to feel the need of re-encompassing the lost exterior world, the forms that began to emerge from the ascendent affirmation of his wild abstractions resembled the tortured inhabitants of the declining world of Soutine.

Expressionism: Munch and Ensor

The word Expressionism as applied to art was originally used to cover only that special movement in Germany before, during and after World War I which gave us the plays of Toller and Brecht, the sculpture of Barlach and Lehmbruck, the painting of Nolde, Kokoschka and Klee, and such a pioneering moving picture as *The Cabinet of Dr. Caligari.* The characteristics which most of the typical works of this movement have in common and which are summed up most exaggeratedly in *Caligari* are an anxiety about the duration and worth of life, accompanied by an equally far-fetched sensitivity to subtle emotions—compassion and love being thought to be never remote from sadism and suicide. But if the high-pitched strains of *Tristan* may be detected in the background of this art, and (with the advantage of hindsight) the flames of the Reichstag and the shrieks of Buchenwald in the foreground, this is not to imply that the artists of German Expressionism were any less humane than their contemporaries elsewhere who saw life in less naked or more abstract terms.

∎

[4] See page 147.

What gave German Expressionism its peculiar flavor from the outset, perhaps, was the discovery of the primitive. The exhibition of tribal totems in other countries, notably France, had an impact mainly stylistic; but in Central and Northern Europe the immediacy of the revelation combined with a current of atavism already in the air to produce an art self-consciously naïve, violently emotional and nihilistic.

The art of the Norwegian painter Edvard Munch, who spent much time in Germany and received his first acclaim there between 1892 and 1908, was one of two major preludes to this development. Munch's art is neither naïve nor primitivistic but it is full of anxiety and high-keyed emotion; this, and the fact that it so conspicuously lacked the orderly restraint of French art, may have been what endeared it so quickly to the Germans.

In the late Eighties and early Nineties Munch spent some time in Paris where he studied the work of Seurat and the Impressionists. He

Munch's "Jealousy" (lithograph, *Collection Museum of Modern Art*). Expressive content via psychological drama. Notice the smoky emotional swirls that burst from the tormented dreamer to envelope his dream.

seems to have become familiar with pictures by Gauguin and Van Gogh on the same visit. From Gauguin he learned how to use flat patterns of color and an abruptly tilted perspective. The swirling skies and expanding ripples of sound that fan out from the open mouth of his "The Cry" to fill the whole universe, are reminiscent of Van Gogh. But Munch was a highly original artist and what distinguishes him from the French school as a whole is that subject-matter—in his case the loves, frustrations and sufferings of his fellow men—is the motive power of his art. Style was the means, and only the means, by which he could best communicate his ideas and feelings about them. From other artists he took what he needed, to say what he had to say, no more. Munch's world is sombre, sometimes bleak, but in it his time lives, and his people have a hectic reality that is unforgettable.

When Munch fails in his paintings it may be in those instances where he relied too heavily on the content of his own life: his disappointments in love, his sicknesses, his isolation from the mainstream of European art. He succeeds in those cases where the times permitted him to be what he wanted to be—a popular artist—without sacrificing his integrity. The finest of Munch's lithographs, the medium through which his art reached its true eloquence, are equalled only by the best of Daumier's; his woodcuts are unsurpassed; and his murals in Oslo in which he deliberately used familiar and popular material in order to reach the broadest public, are said to express uniquely the vigor and hope of the Scandinavian peoples.

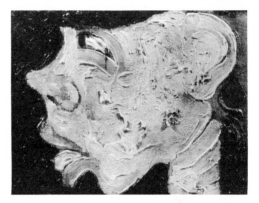

Detail of Ensor's "Entry of Christ into Brussels." Spiritual content masked as allegorical social satire.

The second major prelude to German Expressionism was the fantastic art of the Belgian James Ensor. Ensor died after the conclusion of the Second World War but his major accomplishments and influence date from before the First. Ensor lived something of the life of a recluse in his father's antique shop in Ostend, a seaport where the townspeople on carnival days still wore masks. Without studying Magnasco as Goya had, or going to the South Seas like Gauguin, Ensor therefore stumbled on a device by which he was able to express most effectively his alienation from society. In so doing, he gave the Expressionists, from Nolde to Max Ernst, one of their favorite props.

In another age a moralist like Ensor, who was concerned not only with his personal inability to cope with life but with such social paradoxes as the discrepancy between Christian doctrine and war, would have painted allegories. As it was, even such allegories as Goya managed on occasion seemed unjustified, and Ensor would certainly have agreed with the Spanish artist's mature conclusion that "The dream of reason begets monsters."

Ensor's world is peopled with monsters, monsters of sadism and monsters of indifference. Christ, when he appears in it, is only the archetype of man persecuted. He is Ensor, the unappreciated genius. Ensor even wrote his own name in place of INRI over the Crucifixion—and the name of one of his insensitive critics on the Centurion's lance. His "St. Anthony," unlike Bosch's or Gruenewald's, is a bewildered old man. In his "Baptism" two figures are dunking each other with wash-buckets. Like Callot,[5] whose work he drew upon in much the same way that Klee was later to draw upon his, Ensor found comic fantasy the only means of dealing with disasters seemingly too vast and illogical for tragic treatment. But Ensor's laughter, unlike Callot's, was without humor; and unlike Goya's it was without rage; and unlike Daumier's it was without fellow-feeling.

Expressionism: The German Phase

Meanwhile, separated by only two years, two events had taken place in Germany which established the primitivistic direction of the mainstream of Expressionism. In 1904 Ernst Ludwig Kirchner "discovered"

Nolde's "Head of a Prophet." Religious primitivism of the *Bruecke*. "Perhaps no other single Expressionist print is as deeply emotional, as insistently dramatic, as obviously intense as this powerful head."
—Paul J. Sachs

African and Oceanic art in the cases of the newly established Dresden Ethnological Museum.[6] In 1906 the first book ever written on the expres-

■

[5] See *Callot* by Edwin deT. Bechtel, George Braziller, Inc.

[6] "Where Gauguin had known the Marquesas, and the *fauves* parts of Africa, the Germans, with proper thoroughness, found both Africa and Oceania at once and in a museum; and as befitted the more advanced state of ethnological collecting in their country, they immediately became acquainted with a range and variety of styles which it took the French some years to discover."—Robert J. Goldwater in *Primitivism in Modern Painting*, my principal source of the account of German Expressionism that follows.

sive art of children was translated into German. Although the two principal schools of German Expressionism, the Bruecke of 1906 and the Blaue Reiter of 1912, borrowed from both these sources, the Bruecke was attracted primarily to the exotic and the Blaue Reiter predominantly to the

Klee's "Child Consecrated to Suffering." Children's art as employed expressively by a master of the *Blaue Reiter*.

naïve. It followed that the subject matter of the Bruecke artists tended to be religious, that of the Blaue Reiter "subconscious" and "automatic" though with spiritual overtones.

Consider the subjects of some of the pictures of Nolde, the outstanding painter of the first group. "Woman and Child," "The Missionary," "Excited People," "The Last Supper," "New Guinea Natives" and "Death of Mary of Egypt" are typical titles. Nolde travelled to the South Seas and he admired Gauguin, but it is his *non-formal* use of primitive motives that sets him apart from that artist and from Picasso. In Nolde, the primitive is not idealized. Rather it is used as a means of recapturing and con-

Kollwitz' "Death and the Child" and "Death Tears a Child from its Mother" (lithographs, *Collection Museum of Modern Art*). Limitation of Expressionism in the revolutionary poster that sentimentalizes compassion.

veying directly those religious emotions which animated such of the great expressive arts of the past as the Gothic. In the cabaret scenes, which are among their most frequently painted subjects, the artists of the Bruecke were looking for the same intensity beyond the inexpressive complacencies of everyday life which Biblical subjects afforded. In the latter, as Goldwater remarks, they were attempting "to bring out the essential, the inner

quality of the story, getting rid of everything but the concentrated expression of violent emotion. *The hierarchical, the churchly surface is
stripped off, and a return is made to a primitive Christianity.*" (My italics.)
Less human in its references than Munch's art or Rouault's, less poetic in
its fusion of color and form for emotional effect than Soutine's, the painting of the Bruecke rarely succeeds in transforming its vague emotionalism
into controlled spirituality or its savage sources into more than a blurred
dissonance.

The painting of the Blaue Reiter is at once less ambitious and more
successful. The unfocussed macrocosm of the Bruecke yields to a miniature world of delicate nuances, fascinating particularities, inner percep-
tions. It is a private world, most memorably projected in the minuscule
drawings and well-organized paintings of Paul Klee. Kandinsky, later
to become a patron saint of the biomorphic Non-objectivists,[7] enunciated
the theory on which the Blaue Reiter blossomed in his *The Art of Spiritual
Harmony* (1910): "Like ourselves these artists [the Primitives] sought to
express in their work only internal truths, renouncing in consequence all
consideration of external form." The statement is of dubious veracity but
it indicates the theory on which the neo-primitives based themselves.
Kandinsky not only believed that children are innately capable of portray-
ing externals but that "the talented child has the power to clothe the
abiding inner truth in the form in which this inner truth appears as the
most effective" and that this godlike gift was related to what Christ had
in mind when he said "Suffer the little children to come unto Me, and forbid them not, for of such is the Kingdom of Heaven."[8]

In identifying themselves with simple people, the artists of the Blaue
Reiter went directly to folk art for guidance and in so doing tended superficially to identify their aims with the aspirations of such people. One of
their members, Franz Marc, said that "Artists are the only interpreters and
fulfillers of the will of the people." Deploring the fact that the people at
present did not seem to want much, he looked for a revival of the Mediaeval spirit. Meanwhile, to arrive at this mystical identification with
the universe, Marc, like Kandinsky, tended to paint more and more
abstractly, on the theory that intuition rather than reason was the key to
true simplicity. Only Klee, among the artists identified with the Blaue
Reiter, managed to avoid the amorphous by uniting precariously in his
very personal mysticism elements of both the conscious and unconscious
mind. He remains a minor artist, not because, as the Formalist critic
Thomas Hess maintains, a painter is a seer "only in the form he creates on
the flat surface confronting him," but because, as Emily Genauer suggests,
Klee "perceives without feeling or caring very much."[9]

■

[7] See page 130.

[8] I have already noted (page 57) how Rembrandt returned to the same source for moral
rather than anti-intellectual inspiration.

[9] Hess's opinion of Klee is from a review in *The New York Times* of January 1955, Miss
Genauer's from her column in the *New York Herald Tribune* two months later. These

However far these painters were in the actual practise of their art from fulfilling "the will of the people" (as Marc put it), the fact that they were thinking in this direction and associated themselves, as many including Klee did, with such a socialistic institution as the Bauhaus, indicates the trend German art was taking. Munch had regarded workers as the most important social force of his time and had painted mechanics and masons as symbols of a new force as early as 1908. The two most influential artists of the Twenties in Germany, apart from Klee, were Georg Grosz and Kaethe Kollwitz, both of them identified with the socialist movement.

Grosz is a social satirist whose pessimism, akin to that of Bosch, ideally fitted him to analyze the horrors of war; war is seen as the prelude to civilization's end, and the depraved inheritors of war's aftermath as appropriate participators in an ironic Last Judgment. Grosz's pitiless assault on the spurious romance of city life is conveyed in a nervous broken line that rasps, crawls, cuts and bleeds very well but that could not possibly commiserate or sing. This Expressionist line was suited to prophecies of human perversion that did not seem exaggerated when the asylum of the Third Reich was opened for inspection in 1945, but Grosz's vision is too limited by the narrowness of his contempt to have implications beyond the documentary.

Kollwitz's world is even more limited in its subject-matter than Grosz's—starving children, loving but tragic mothers, and workers heroic in defeat—but it is occasionally lifted out of time and place by a monumental compassion. The masses and heavy accents of her drawing derive from Munch, but behind that her strength stems from the tradition of Western religious art. Her grandfather, Julius Rupp, founded the first free religious congregation in Germany in 1846. She received religious instruction from him as a child, but noted: "A loving God was never brought home to me. . . . I venerated Him, but I loved Jesus. My father . . . introduced me to socialism, socialism understood as the much-desired Brotherhood of Man. Behind him stood Rupp, a being linked not to men but to God." Hogarth's illustrations impressed Kollwitz early in life; then Rembrandt, whose practise of making studies from himself she followed. Carl Zigrosser says that a year in Italy failed to weaken Kollwitz toward idealization. Her work, like Barlach's though less stylized, remained essentially Gothic, emotional, expressive, and like Daumier's more universal as time passed.

But again we are confronted by the fatality that so often seems to pursue the modern artist for whom content is central. She was confined by that preoccupation to a single obsessive image, and finally, in her old age, to an almost monastic withdrawal from both life and art. It is true, as Zigrosser says in his monograph on her lithographs,[10] that Kollwitz was

■

critics, whose divergent opinions confirm the divergent poles of this book, are quoted extensively in the Epilogue.

[10] *Kaethe Kollwitz* edited with an Introduction by Carl Zigrosser, Chicago, Bittner-Regnery, 1946.

not motivated by the revolutionary class struggle or by allegiance to any party but by social conscience and humanitarianism; nevertheless there is a dreary monotony about her suffering types, and the sentiment in such a print as "Woman Welcoming Death" approaches dangerously close to sentimentality. Why is this so? And why did Kollwitz through the years of Nazism and War fall back on a non-productive "serenity"? The answer is partly in the times—the atomized Europe of the Twentieth Century which provided no common meeting ground for revolutionary content and

Beckmann's "Christ and the Woman Taken in Adultery." In its adaptation of North German Gothic, this was as close as German Expressionism came to relating the nihilism of the times to the great expressive tradition.

revolutionary form. It is partly in the socialist movement which has always lacked the imagination to employ an artist of Kollwitz' stature for posters personifying more than defeat and death. And it is partly, of course, in Kollwitz' own lack of imagination and will.

Only Beckmann among the German Expressionists created a style that transcends its origins, a style that cries out for walls but never found a public. In the Germany between the wars Beckmann was fighting his way clear of cults—especially the primitivism of the Bruecke that would have liked to claim him. As a young man he had bowed before Rembrandt for his humanity and before Piero della Francesca for his mastery of form. But it was a view of the late Gothic masterpiece, the "Villeneuve Pietà" in the Louvre, that gave Beckmann a hint of a direction. That, and the shock of the War, which convinced him, a participant, that nothing said on a small scale or in a private language would measure up to the enormities of his time as he had witnessed them. Beckmann now painted the "Crucifixion" (twice), "The Woman Taken in Adultery," "Bathsheeba" and "The Battle of the Amazons." He even attempted to convey the immediate impact of such recent events as the "Messina Earthquake" and "The Sinking of the Titanic." War's suppression of the individual had made Beckmann look for a code language that would say big things without causing a strain for mere magnitude. In an adaptation of North German Gothic—the harsh wounded features, the elongated rubbery limbs— he found it.

Everything in Beckmann is larger than life—the personalities, the landscapes, the emotions, the symbols—everything but the communicative content. That is always suppressed. His sympathy hides behind the archaic grimace, his will to freedom behind the ambiguous gesture. In the easy-going Germany of the Weimar Republic he had dealt obliquely with the bestialities to come. Under Hitler he spoke perforce in parables, hiding his "Departure" in an attic and entitling it "Scenes from Shakespeare's Tempest." In the New World he painted Old World allegories: expressive triptychs for formalist museums, denunciations of power for millionaires' collections. "I am seeking," he said, "for the bridge which leads from the visible to the invisible." Blake, in a dream, told him how, but not where, to find it. "Have confidence in objects," he said. "Do not let yourself be intimidated by the horror of the world."

Orozco's High-Pitched Voice

It is surely one of the ironies of the age that the only country willing to enlist the capacities of a major artist from birth to death, and with a public interested enough in art to give such an artist the inspiration of recognition as the peer of statesmen, should be "backward" Mexico.

Where else today but in Mexico could an artist of Orozco's stature have produced a body of work quantitatively so staggering and ultimately (through the opportunities of communicative cross-fertilization) so satisfying? Mexico, in the years preceding the mural renaissance of 1922, was far enough from Europe to have a popular tradition of its own, but not too far to prevent a great artist from eventually borrowing what he needed from his contemporaries. As a nation in the throes of a social revolution, Mexico gave its artists a sense of belonging to and working for the people —and the future. As a country of Spanish culture, even its provincial schools were not insensible to the spirit of Greco and Goya. But above all Orozco and his vigorous compatriots were fortunate in inheriting the *humanistic* revolt against academicism which painting took in Mexico—in glaring contrast to the purely formalistic revolt which was still going on in the Paris of Manet, Gauguin, Seurat, Matisse and Picasso.

As a young man, Orozco attended classes at the San Carlos Academy where he learned nothing except a respect for Mexican subject-matter and, perhaps from the example of Julio Ruelas, confirmation of a taste he had already developed for pictures of bawdy-houses and the macabre. Orozco's real masters were José Guadalupe Posada and Dr. Atl.

Posada was the fabulous print-maker whose 15,000 engravings, comparable at their best to those of Goya and Daumier, and stemming directly from Mexican folk art, had already given Orozco his basic direction. One of this great draftsman's folk-symbols was the *calavera,* or animated skele-

Posada's "End of the World." A great popular engraver's vision of a mad world careening to catastrophe that was to inspire Orozco.

ton, who, carrying on all the sensual, comic and brutish activities of day-to-day life, is there to remind one of its inevitable end. Another of Posada's preoccupations was the dishonesty of businessmen and politicians under the Francophile dictatorship of Porfirio Diaz. Orozco was never to lose Posada's sense of a mad world careening to catastrophe.

Dr. Atl, who had just returned from Italy, was the theoretical leader of the younger artists. From him Orozco gained the conviction that it was art's function to express the human conflicts of the present with all the resources of the past. The apprentice stage of Orozco's life came to a close, significantly, when his fellow-students (led by Siqueiros who went to jail for actually stoning the professors) organized a strike *in protest against a new French system for teaching children to draw abstractly.*

One reason, and a symbolic one, why Orozco stood somewhat aloof from the violent revolutionary events of 1910-15 was that as a boy he had lost the use of his left hand and in part his eyesight as the result of an experiment with gunpowder. During the revolution, while Madero, Huerta,

Carranza and Villa were betraying their followers in their various ways, Orozco painted prostitutes, drunken half-breeds and generals gambling with government funds. He even caricatured the incorruptible Zapata on the grounds, as he later stated, that "everything was the same and re-

Orozco's "St. Francis and the Indian." Expressive content reaching a new peak in an image for which one must go back as far as Giotto to find a parallel for monumental conviction.

mained the same as before the uprising." His biographer, MacKinley Helm, thinks that the moral burden of the years of monumental painting that followed "derived from Orozco's war-begot apprehension of the dualism of barbarity on the one side of humankind, as he knew it, and of pathos on the other." [11] Jezebel alone among Orozco's figures escapes this tension between terror and pity. His earliest symbolic figure, she screams with laughter as she grows into the Fallen Woman Triumphant. We forgive her, says Helm, "because she saved her creator from the pitfall of sentimentality, the most dangerous trap in the way of an artist with feeling."

Orozco resembles Michelangelo in style as well as in temperament. Like Michelangelo, the great Mexican was a violently unorthodox but essentially religious painter. Indifferent to landscape and nature, cavalier with color, contemptuous of decorative "taste" in fitting mural design to architecture, both artists use the human body, tortured by political ambition or warped by disease, as the vehicle for expressing colossal anger and pity in the face of man's inhumanity. Like Goya and Daumier, Orozco compounds feeling and farce in such a way as to avoid the limitations of even so fine a "proletarian" artist as Kollwitz. Hogarth's provincial caricature is as remote from him by reason of his conviction that the poetry of painting takes place two-dimensionally. In linear terms, this conviction is apparent as early as the National Preparatory School frescoes of 1922. In terms of color, it was confirmed by the rediscovery of his affinity with El Greco's Baroque extravagance, a revelation which took place during his first trip to Europe just before the experimental Dartmouth mural of 1932. Helm thinks that on that trip Orozco may also have borrowed from the Tintoretto of San Rocco two principles he was later to put into practice in the dome of Guadalajara. For it was there that he first gave his figures space in which to move about, without losing them "behind" the picture-plane; and it was there that they first take on that extraordinary "continuity" of action which in Tintoretto has been compared to Eisenstein's cinematic montage.

Like Daumier and Goya, and unlike Tintoretto and Rouault, Orozco was not himself a practicing Christian. He told his sons that men have mystical potentialities which they ought to cultivate in private. His painting is from beginning to end the record of his own search for spiritual truth in the brutal history of his time. It was no accident that when the Mexicans started symbolizing the revolution in paint, every one of them, including the Communist Siqueiros, fell back on traditional Christian iconography. Orozco himself painted the Virgin—and was shocked that the public considered painting her nude as blasphemous. He had planned to represent Christ in a subsequent panel, and he did paint Him many times thereafter. In one fresco Christ is destroying his Cross in despair over its misuse as a symbol. In another (the Dartmouth version) Christ emerges from a landscape of tanks, howitzers and shattered idols, axe in hand, the right fist clenched, like the Destroyer of Michelangelo's "Last Judgment," to accuse mankind of betrayal. But the images of spiritual truth that remain with us longest are not those of terror and rage but of anguish and

■

[11] *Man of Fire: J. C. Orozco, An Interpretative Biography* by MacKinley Helm, New York, Harcourt, Brace, 1953.

Orozco's "Migration." Michelangelo or his master Signorelli is recalled in the muscular rhythms of this major chord to mankind indomitable.

pity: the Franciscan Father enveloping the starved Indian in his embrace, Father Hidalgo unforgettably mourning amid handcuffed prisoners as he writes the word LIBERTY on a scroll.

Propaganda or Abstraction?

In Orozco, sustained as he was by this vision of the spiritual and by the plastic example of the masters of expressive content, there is infrequent descent into the banalities of propaganda. Such awkward painting as the New England scenes in the Dartmouth mural may be traced to the simple mistake of trying to deal with material wholly foreign to his background. But such occasional lapses, recalling as they do the less inspired discursive panels of Diego Rivera in the Ministry of Education and elsewhere, call for a word on the subject of modern mural painting in general.

Schmeckebier, in his extended analysis of the Mexican mural movement,[12] contrasts the structural design that governs Orozco's work even in caricature with the extent to which Rivera and the lesser muralists depend on *association* (in the eye of the observer) for their effect. Thus a worker will be characterized by a radiant smile, an exploiter by a scowl,

■

[12] *Modern Mexican Art* by Laurence E. Schmeckebier, 1939.

etc. "The mural may act as a stimulant, but that stimulation is one of recognition rather than of new constructive thought." This weakness is occasionally disturbing in the frescoes of the Ministry of Education and the National Palace where decorative ingenuity goes a long way, narrative is not obtrusive and individual figures, even such a stock one as the hypocritically weeping cleric, are really painted. But in the murals for the Hotel Reforma and most of those executed in the United States, content on the lowest illustrative and even literary level displaces form altogether.

Rivera's influence in the United States in the Thirties raises the question of the failure of American social art to rise even to his not inconsiderable accomplishment. Why did the WPA Arts Project, for instance, with its laudable commissioning of 1300 murals and 48,100 oils, fail so signally

Rivera's "Priest" (detail of fresco). A plausible and boldly communicative anti-clerical symbol soon to become an aesthetically empty stock figure of propaganda.

to raise American representational art beyond the level of reportage? The answer is, perhaps, that it did—but too late. By the time Ben Shahn was starting to paint his expressive mural in the new Social Security Building in Washington in 1940,[13] the project had been liquidated and the War begun. By the time such WPA artists as Rico Lebrun, Willem de Kooning, Morris Graves, Jack Levine and Hyman Bloom had begun to discover their mature styles and their relation to the history of painting, the War was over—and with it any thought that the government would again become a patron of the arts. President Truman of Missouri was comparing modern art to scrambled eggs and President Eisenhower of Kansas was asking Bobby Jones to approve his putting stance in a portrait of the golfer he had just copied from a press photograph.

The murals actually painted in post offices and federal buildings from 1933 to 1939 were the tired swan song of a tradition of factual realism in

■

[13] Shahn's evolution from realistic reportage to monumental lyricism to expressive content in his three murals is an evolution the government art projects themselves might have experienced if extended. See my *Portrait of the Artist as an American*, pp. 69-110, for an account of this phase of Shahn's work and of his association with Diego Rivera.

America that had had its golden age in the painting of Thomas Eakins and Winslow Homer and its popularization a generation or two later in the work of such vigorous journeymen as George Bellows, Boardman Robinson and Thomas Hart Benton. The styles of A. P. Ryder and Marsden Hartley, the only American expressionists of real originality in their time, and of John Marin, our first Formalist, were unsuited to mural painting, even had Ryder been living then, and Marin and Hartley, at sixty-five and sixty-three, willing.

To return to Orozco, as early as 1930, when he was in New York working on the murals in the New School for Social Research, he had been thrown off the track (his track) by the mirage of an "objective" art. He had fallen sway to the theory of dynamic symmetry as propounded in the treatises of a Canadian theorist, Jay Hambidge. Hambidge had believed

Hartley's "Fisherman's Last Supper." In a world of quick profits, cheap faiths and forgotten myths, the expressive artist may live like a recluse and be drawn to the primitive. Hartley's tongue-tied people (to quote his description of them) "are pretty much like children" and "go to their death without murmur and without reproach."

the relation between static and dynamic forms to be calculable, and the drawings Orozco made while persuaded of the plausibility of this fantastic theory are a key to the atypical, non-ecstatic forms in his unsuccessful New York mural. Later, in Paris, he had been impressed and disturbed by an exhibition of the latest Picassos. He sensed there, perhaps, a vitality lacking in most of those travelling his way. Later, in 1940, Orozco was torn from one of his most expressive works, the great black-and-white battle scenes at Jiquilpan, to paint six portable panels for the Museum of Modern Art as a public demonstration of how the Mexicans painted their murals. The result, "Dive-Bomber," is probably the coldest of Orozco's works, and the explanation of it he wrote for the Museum is as abstract and uninspired as the mural itself. Helm observes wryly that Orozco was not at home with the "subjectless object," and adds:

117

He had hitherto filled small left-over spaces with object (as against subject) motifs, but now he thought he would try a big object painting; he said, we know, that the six big panels could be shown in any casual order. But the formalist effort failed to come off effectively. Its content was simply not interesting enough to engage the attention. Orozco had gone to the newest of churches but he sat uneasily in a stranger's pew. He had grown up and reached his maturity in a milieu in which sound doctrine had it that painting, at least by intention, must play a useful and not merely an entertaining part in the national culture.

Almost Orozco's last work was the abstract-symbolic painting in ethyl silicate on the six-story concrete wall behind the stage of the new National Normal School in Mexico City. Work on it interrupted his completion of an "Apocalypse" in the Temple of Jesus at Guadalajara and preceded an equally characteristic frieze, unfinished at the time of his death but described in effect when he wrote "My theme is humanity, my drift is emotion, my means the real and integral representation of bodies." The huge mural abstraction, an illegible pastiche of Léger and Picasso, need only be compared with such a luminously alive late work as the "Stoning of St. Stephen" for one to be reminded concretely where Orozco's heart lay. He had revealed it in words in a letter to a friend:

> Error and exaggeration do not matter. What matters is boldness in thinking with a high-pitched voice; in speaking out about things as one feels them in the moment of speaking; in having the temerity to proclaim what one believes to be true without fear of the consequences . . . If one were to await the possession of the absolute truth, one must be either a fool or a mute. If the creative impulse were muted, the world would then be stayed on its march.

The Religion of Form: Matisse

We left the dominant succession of formalist painting with Gauguin —Gauguin hurrying away from the madness of his expressionist friend in Arles to the "pure" atmosphere of the Marquesas, where he could paint a native model on a sofa, and then, under the spell of that form and those colors, discover the "content" of the picture in the afterthought of a bedside ghost and an exotic title.

It was to be the ghost of a content with a short life. For Gauguin's successor and the master spirit of formalist painting from Gauguin's time to our own would dispense with it from the outset of his career, not returning to it until fifty years later in the twilight of his life when the bare walls of a Christian chapel would challenge that hand, so tirelessly prolific of lyrical decorations, to invent symbols.

Matisse's first stirrings as a painter are as unimpulsive, as logical, and as hypothetically French as a devoted worshipper of Continental taste could ask. But only a German professor could have followed with a scholarship as exhaustive as Alfred Barr's [14] the minute deviations and intricate ramifications of a style that in Matisse's case *is* the man. This book, with its 592 double-column pages and its hundreds of plates, records every move in the life of an artist whose aim was to be motionless and to paint pictures, as he himself put it, "free of disturbing subject matter—like a

Orozco's "Stoning of St. Stephen." Scripture and myth revitalized in the luminous reality of *now*. "What matters is thinking with a high-pitched voice . . ."

comfortable armchair in which one can recover from physical fatigue." The result is as unanswerable as a dictionary and as dull as a seed-catalogue.

What slight shifts in Matisse's essentially uniform manner have occurred, Barr traces with the acumen of a Sherlock Holmes reconstructing a whole crime from a single hair. If what results is less than hair-raising, it has all the grace of one of the artist's odalisques:

> Though the *Blue Still-Life* is one of Matisse's most beautiful paintings it seems essentially retrospective in character if compared with the *Pink Onions* or the *Asphodels*. The fluid handling of the decorated surfaces, certain color passages, even the technical variety are more or less fauve in spirit but the rather conven-

■

[14] *Matisse: His Art and His Public* by Alfred H. Barr, Jr., New York, Museum of Modern Art, 1951.

tional dignity in the composition and the density of the objects seem far closer to Cézanne than to most of Matisse's paintings of the year before or the year following.

Being mainly a description of such pictures and their variations one from another, Barr's book has more to say about wealthy collectors and their collections than about the life of an artist in a country recovering from the brunt of the greatest war in history only to be plunged into a greater:

> In all ways Matisse's life seems to have been calm and regularly ordered during the 1920s. He was now highly successful on an economic as well as an artistic level, a great asset to his principal dealers Bernheim-Jeune, with whom he had made his fourth three-year contract late in 1920 at increased prices, Appendix C. His paintings of the years 1920-1925 appear to be perfect expressions of a serene, industrious and uneventful life, pages 434-443. Girls looking out of the window or playing the piano or violin in the apartment at Nice, or girls costumed as odalisques in oriental pantaloons and embroidered jackets, or nude, standing before patterned textiles or tiled screens, lolling on rug-strewn divans; still-lifes of fruit and flowers, richly furnished interiors in which a dozen different colors, textures and patterned surfaces are magically harmonized in a hedonistic, sensual and charming art with no challenging or difficult moments—except for the painter.

When Matisse takes off for Tahiti in 1930 one's pulse quickens. At last, one thinks, the artist has become bored with re-arranging his arrangements, clarifying his palette and re-interpreting Cézanne. He wants to see how a different order of human beings lives, or at least what they look like. But no. Nothing could be further from the fact. "I have always been taken," Matisse wrote to a friend after returning, "with the character of the light which bathes the objects of my contemplation, and often I had asked myself during my meditations, what would be the particular quality of light in the Antipodes? I stayed there three months, absorbed by my surroundings, without a thought in my head . . ."

Let me interject at this point that it is not the painter, or his right to bathe himself in the light of the Antipodes, that I take exception to, but his deification by intellectual taste; not to the biographer, but to his book as a symbol of that deification. For talent and integrity Matisse has had few superiors among the world's influential painters; and among art critics Barr writes with a sobriety and discernment that are beyond reproach.

Matisse's career begins in the early 1890s when he became a pupil of Gustave Moreau and made a living by copying paintings by Poussin and Chardin for the government. During this decade, interiors and still-lifes were almost his only subjects. In his own work he was influenced by the Impressionists and Gauguin; but the big event of Matisse's artistic life (which is to say, of his life) was his discovery and purchase from Vollard of a small Cézanne. Cézanne's "Bathers," we are told, completely eclipsed for him Van Gogh's "l'Arlésienne" at the same gallery, and seemed, in comparison with a Sisley there, "a moment of the artist" as against "a moment of nature." Barr is at pains to pin down exactly what it was Matisse got out of Cézanne, but he does not altogether succeed. Matisse was fascinated by the timeless, unlocalized quality of the master of Aix, and by his capacity to make life-long variations on the same theme. But the Fauves of 1905, of whom Matisse was the acknowledged leader, were more influenced by the romanticism of Gauguin and by African sculpture and children's drawings, than by Cézanne, and the motivation of their painting, with its deliberately harsh outlines, emotionally contrasted bright colors and unlocalized scene, was the conveying of an immediate, over-all impact. "What I am after, above all," wrote Matisse in 1908, "is expression. . . . Expression in my way of thinking does not consist of the passion mirrored upon a human face or betrayed by a violent gesture. The whole arrangement of my picture is expressive."

All the subsequent art of Matisse represents the attempt to synthesize this instinctual response to visual reality with the architectonic equilibrium of Cézanne. The variations in his style may be traced to fluctuations in these two impulses: the will to indulge in liberating experiment, though always formal, vs. the need for discipline and security. Whereas in Van Gogh, and even to a certain extent in Gauguin, the colors and figures

Matisse's "Icarus" from *Jazz* (*Courtesy Museum of Modern Art*). In these cut-out paper decorations the human figure still plays a part, but not humanity. Penultimate station on the main line to Non-objectivism.

which form patterns are juxtaposed for psychological reasons, in Matisse the visual-pictorial effect is everything. In fact, a studied attempt is made to *dis*relate the figures in a landscape one from another in order to heighten the scene's particularity *as a painting*. Put philosophically, there are objects in Matisse but no subjects. The difference separating this art from pure abstraction is very slight, and one is not surprised to find Matisse—in the cut-out-paper forms of *Jazz* (1944-45)—experimenting with nonobjective shapes. It may seem more surprising that the so-called Nonobjective painters in New York in the late Forties came to regard Matisse rather than Picasso as their true master; but this may be explained when we come to consider Picasso's deviations from formalism. Besides, as Barr reminds us,

> Such men as Pollock, Baziotes, de Kooning, Motherwell and the late Arshile Gorky, in spite of the abstract appearance of their paintings . . . did not think of themselves as abstract painters. Far more than their work indicated they were striving for an art in which natural forms, including human figures, would once more *emerge* but without any sacrifice of spontaneity, or of the direct impact, purity and reality of the painted surface as the primary instrument of their emotions. For these American painters as well as their French colleagues Matisse began to have a special significance.

I shall return to Matisse, who painted in his eighty-second year the decorations for the Dominican chapel at Vence, when considering the

Matisse's "Joy of Life." Objects but no subjects. Figures in a landscape deliberately disrelated to heighten the scene's particularity as painting.

future of Formalism at the conclusion of this chapter. Meanwhile, this is the place to discuss the less single-minded but even more influential evolution of Matisse's great rival and contemporary, Picasso.

Picasso's "Demoiselles d'Avignon" (*Collection Museum of Modern Art*). The picture that ushered in Cubism and the arts of geometric abstraction. Primitive African and Iberian fetishes provided the vocabulary but not the script.

The Religion of Form: Picasso

Shortly after Matisse had finished the climactic picture of his first phase, the "Joy of Life" now in the Barnes Collection at Merion, Pennsylvania, Picasso began work on a huge canvas summarizing his quite different research into problems of form, the so-called "Demoiselles d'Avignon," now in the collection of the Museum of Modern Art. Barr, who has written a study of Picasso almost as exhaustive as his treatise on Matisse, tells the story of the painting of this most influential of modern pictures in both books.[15] The point of greatest interest is that the two paintings, different

■

[15] *Picasso: Fifty Years of His Art* by Alfred H. Barr, Jr., New York, Museum of Modern Art, 1946.

though they are in spirit and form, have their common origin in the "Bathers" of Cézanne. The other sources of Matisse's flowing, decorative bacchanale were Ingres, Puvis de Chavannes, Corot, and further back Poussin and Giorgione. The additional (and immediate) source of Picasso's major picture of 1907 was the current "discovery" of primitive sculpture, in Picasso's case archaic Iberian as well as West African. Matisse's graceful eclogue was destined to become a principal source of the "organic" or "biomorphic" abstractions of Kandinsky and Miró, Gorky and Baziotes. Picasso's seemingly so different *fête champêtre* of angular giantesses, frightening in their frontality, was to become the inspiration of Cubism, and later on of all the arts of geometrical abstraction from Malevich and Mondrian to Abraham Rattner, Ben Nicholson and George L. K. Morris.

Picasso, who was only twenty-five at the time, had already exhausted the possibilities of several styles, any one of which would have occupied a less ambitious artist for a lifetime. Born with the inventiveness of a Goya and the facility of a Raphael, Picasso was already well on his way to producing an art that in its chameleon changes and denial of human warmth perfectly reflected its time. Among painters of comparable endowment—and history has not many to offer—Picasso is unique for the number of influences that have affected his work. Among these his own contemporaries are few, and borrowings from them are negligible. In addition to those already cited, Picasso has been influenced at various times by Antonio Pollaiuolo, Uccello, Raphael, Gruenewald, Arcimbaldo, Gothic glass and American weathervanes, Greek and Hellenistic sculpture, Romanesque capitals, Etruscan bronzes, Bushman drawing, El Greco, Poussin, Zurbaran, Goya, David, Ingres, Cézanne, Seurat, Lautrec, Puvis de Chavannes, Henri Rousseau, Rodchenko, Miró, de Chirico and Matisse. But the list is as nothing compared to the number of modern artists who have been influenced by Picasso, an influence that began with the "Demoiselles" and shows no sign of abating. What draws other rootless spirits to Picasso (it is significant that the Spanish artist has spent all his mature life in cosmopolitan exile) is his compulsion to "try anything"—a compulsion in which he generally succeeds and the less talented fail—but behind this there has been a general anxiety generated by the conviction that Picasso will have exhausted the possibilities of one style and passed on to another before his rivals and imitators have caught up with the last.

Picasso's is an art derived from other arts. Life, if we except the personality of the artist himself, plays little part in it. When Picasso paints Gertrude Stein, one is looking primarily at an Iberian mask, though the resemblance to the literary abstractionist is not forgotten. When Picasso paints a bull, it is the cave-drawings of Altamira that come to mind, or Goya's "Tauromachy." Even the blue in his famous Blue Period is adapted from Cézanne, as the faces are from Lautrec and others, and the sentiment from Verlaine. The linear portraits of Vollard, Apollinaire, Strawinsky, etc. prove that Picasso can present character as well as anyone if he chooses, but these drawings are exceptional and themselves reflect a fleeting preoccupation with Ingres which may simply have carried with it something of that painter's interest in personality as well as his classicism.

The Evolution of "Guernica"

With the painting of the undramatic "Saltimbanques" of 1905, Picasso "cleanses" his pictures of even the bohemian pathos of the Blue Period which may in some slight degree have reflected the trials and poverty of his early life as an artist. From then on until the controversial pictures touched off by the Spanish Civil War in 1938, Picasso's paintings and his bewildering changes of style reflect nothing but aesthetic discoveries—and their successive exhaustions. The evolution of Cubism from the Negroid "Demoiselles" and from those landscapes of Braque derived from Cézanne's admonition to look in nature for the sphere, the cylinder and the cone, is known to every student of modern art. But it is well to remember, in tracing the dominance of a formalist aesthetic over *both* major Twentieth Century strains, that the Fauvist declaration of art's complete independence of nature had just as much to do with Cubism's theoretical basis as the Space-Time jargon of the period which made the Cubists' attempt to present several aspects of an object simultaneously seem worth while.

For an artist of Picasso's mercurial disposition, Cubism, with its puritanical geometricism and denial of color, was soon *passé*. It remained an instrument in his music room to be taken down and played upon from time to time, but no more. He was content to let his friend Juan Gris exploit it for pattern's sake. A Russian mystic like Malevich and a Dutch savant like Mondrian could carry it to its logical (and arid) conclusion. Embellishing Cubism with snips of paper and capital letters (symbolizing "reality"), with pure color and pointillist backgrounds, might offer sufficient variations to keep a sensuous painter of relatively low voltage like Braque occupied for a lifetime. Picasso has never been interested in decoration for its own sake. Behind such of his pictures as seem to have a primarily decorative value is always the object, and behind the object the aesthetic concept. Thus, his neo-classicism of 1920 may be explained as a reaction against the intellectual excesses of Cubism. He would show that he could outdraw Poussin and Ingres—and he did. Similarly, his "psychologically disturbing" pictures of 1925-27, beginning with the "Three Dancers," followed directly the publication of André Breton's *Surrealist Manifesto* of 1924, taking into account also the exhibition of de Chirico's dream pictures of 1910-17 and a widespreading interest in Freud's analysis of sexual fantasies.

It would be singular if an artist so sensitive to every current in the world of ideas and art as Picasso should not have attempted to bring expressionism itself within the boundaries of his formalist world. The answer is that he did. How well he succeeded, however, depends on whether one defines expressionism as the artistic embodiment of a deep-seated concern with the human and spiritual, or whether it be construed merely as the rendering of forms in aspects of emotional tension. In the second sense, having to do with such an art as we have already examined in James Ensor, Picasso succeeded brilliantly. In the first sense of the word, Picasso would seem to have little in common with the masters of expressive content.

125

Picasso's "Crucifixion" (*Owned by the Artist, Courtesy Museum of Modern Art*). As in the non-secular pictures of Perugino, Poussin and Gauguin, religious subject matter does not necessarily make for spiritual feeling or expressive communication.

It is interesting that the first of the four works which some critics take to identify Picasso with expressionism should have been painted in the first year of the Great Depression: 1930 was the year the Austrian Credit Anstalt failed, precipitating Hitler into prominence in Germany and touching off a wave of strikes and administrative scandals in France. 1930 also happens to be the year Picasso painted his "Crucifixion." The "Crucifixion" is one of Picasso's least successful pictures. The effort to deal with a subject so encrusted with tradition brought out none of his genius for simplification. The composition is hopelessly confused and the iconographical elements are so exaggerated in the attempt to avoid sentiment or repetition that the picture is dominated by a gigantic sponge and two enormous clasped hands. (The latter are said to have been suggested by the Isenheim altarpiece.) As far as feeling goes, even Barr, though he praises the picture's "richness of invention," admits that it "seems entirely devoid of religious significance."

The "Minotauromachy" of 1935, Picasso's most elaborate etching, is expressionist in intent though again Barr is hard put to it to say what it means. "Apparently," he writes, "the scene is a moral melodramatic charade of the soul"—whatever that may be. The picture is dominated by a menacing bull. Facing the Minotaur is a little girl holding a bouquet of flowers in one hand and a candle in the other. Between them a gutted horse careens with a female matador, breasts bared, across its back. On the extreme left a bearded man in a loincloth is climbing a ladder to safety, while from a window in the background two girls and a brace of doves contemplate the scene below. Is the Minotaur Evil and the fearless flower girl the Innocence that will overcome it? Is the ladder-climber the carpenter of the Crucifixion still engaged in his work? Is the horse a symbol of war's victims and the two girls the indifferent spectators of modern tragedy? The etching suggests emotions but is unemotional. One admires and speculates but is not moved.

Whether one was intended to be moved or not, there is no question that in the series of etchings "The Dream and Lie of Franco" that followed, and in "Guernica" which summed up both works, Picasso had every intention of striking a blow for human rights. The series of etchings were printed as postcards and sold for the benefit of the Spanish Republican government. The big black-and-white painting was begun two days after the "experimental" obliteration bombing of Guernica by the Nazis on April 28, 1937. It was intended to be a mural for the Spanish Building at the Paris World's Fair. While working on it, Picasso wrote: "The Spanish struggle is the fight of reaction against the people, against freedom. My whole life as an artist has been nothing more than a continuous struggle against reaction and the death of art . . . and in all my recent works of

Picasso's "Minotauromachy" (*Collection Museum of Modern Art*). In this prodigious etching, the imagery of which was to be incorporated in "Guernica," content is expressive but hermetic.

art I clearly express my abhorrence of the military caste which has sunk Spain in an ocean of pain and death."

The question has often been asked: Without a knowledge of Picasso's politics would anyone respond to the communicative intention of the etchings and the mural? The fact that the question has been asked more often by the enemies of art than by its friends does not affect its relevance. We are forced to conclude that the honest answer is: No. As propaganda [16] the etchings deriding Franco are as meaningless—and as childish—as the surrealist "poem" that Picasso wrote to accompany them. "Fandango owl souse of swords of evil-omened polyps scouring brush of hairs from priests' tonsures standing naked in the middle of the frying pan," etc., etc. Franco is depicted as a hairy polyp killing a monstrous horse—presumably the Spanish people—and being killed in turn by a bison-headed bull—this time, apparently, the spirit of Good. To get anything explicit out of the

Picasso's "Guernica" (*Owned by the Artist, Courtesy Museum of Modern Art*). Climactic picture of the first half of the Twentieth Century. Expressionism and Formalism join, though the result is expressive without being communicative, formal without being mannered.

similar symbolism of "Guernica" one must be familiar not only with "Minotauromachy," but with the whole evolution of Picasso's art. Even then the meaning is far from clear.

The further question arises: Is it art? Unequivocally: Yes. In formal terms, "Guernica" is the most impressive of Picasso's semi-abstract constructions. It is a miracle of dissonant composition and multiple invention. In such terms it stands comparison with Uccello's great battle-scenes, Pollaiuolo's "Battle of the Nudes," Tintoretto's "Capture of Zara," Poussin's

■

[16] I use the word advisedly—in the sense that Giotto's "Pietà" is effective propaganda for Christianity and Goya's "Disasters of War" for peace.

"Triumph of Neptune and Amphitrite," David's "Battle of the Romans and the Sabines" and Ensor's "Entry of Christ into Brussels." Among Picasso's works it is unique for a vague but unmistakable emotional intensity. This, while it does not give the picture the communicative power of true expressive content, does take it as far beyond the limits of formalism as the violently agitated pictures of Tintoretto and Ensor mentioned above.

Behind the limitations of the "Guernica" is that sentence of Gauguin's which is supposed to have summed up his aesthetic: "I have gone far back, farther than the horses of the Parthenon . . . as far back as the Dada of my babyhood, the good rocking-horse." It brings one to the point where one is obliged to ask: What next? If "Guernica" is at once the summation and the breaking point of Picasso's art, the point at which Formalism reaches out for expressive content with only the fragmented symbols of archaism and children's art to sustain its message, then the Catholic chapels of Assy and Vence are the outward manifestations of modern art's abhorrence of the aesthetic vacuum of pure form and of its desperate attempt to come to grips with some reality beyond the artist's ego.

Assy and Vence

In 1937 Father Coutourier, a Dominican monk who was also a painter, initiated the movement to bring back to the Church in France the creative vitality of earlier Christian art. To the decoration of the Dominican church at Assy in the French Alps he invited Rouault to design windows, Lurçat to execute a huge tapestry, Lipschitz and Braque to make sculptures, Matisse to outline a St. Dominic on tiles, and Chagall to contribute a series of panels dealing with the Baptism. After the War it was Father Coutourier again who abetted Matisse in his project of designing and entirely carrying out the decoration of the Dominican chapel at Vence on the French Riviera. This project was completed and dedicated in 1950 and Matisse considered it his masterpiece.

Admittedly both chapels have been "successful" to the extent that they have brought works of inventive quality and aesthetic inspiration back into a religious institution for some generations opposed to any manifestations of a living art. They have also succeeded in the sense of giving pleasure to those art lovers who have visited them, and possibly many others through reproductions. It is my contention, however, that these works, and similar religious decorations designed more recently by the Non-objective artists of New York, fail [17] as completely to express values in accordance with the Christian faith as the WPA murals of 1933-39 for the most part failed to give expressive content to democracy or social revolution. The paradox of disbelieving artists in the service of institutions of belief was admitted by Father Coutourier himself when he announced that he "trusted to genius without worrying about religious affinities." Catholic orthodoxy or practicing Christianity is beside the point, of course.

∎

[17] I am prepared to assume (though I have not been able to see reproductions of them) that the windows of Rouault are an exception to this statement.

One can conceive of few painters in history capable of painting a "truer" (in the deepest Christian sense) Crucifixion than the professed atheist Daumier or the agnostic Orozco. The point is rather that most of the painters involved in Assy were, by the very nature of their art, *anti*-religious, anti-expressive. Léger and Lurçat, whose works dominate Assy, were, as a matter of fact, both practicing members of the Communist party, though even this would have not necessarily disqualified them had their work remotely reflected that communal spirit of man's brotherhood which is part of Christ's teaching and which is at least supposed to be a tenet of Marxian socialism. Léger's work, on the contrary, has always been noted for a hard, mechanical precision, and Lurçat's for decorative qualities, both painters being abstractionists. Léger's mosaic, apart from its lettered slogans, would be as appropriate for a Roman Bath as for a Church. Lurçat's tapestry would make an excellent curtain for a ballet on a Mithraic or Aztec theme.

Matisse's views of his work at Vence have been pretty thoroughly reported. In presenting the finished work to the Bishop, Matisse said that he expected it to be judged as "an effort which issues from a life consecrated to truth." He made no explicit reference to religion. In an interview later he had answered the question whether he believed in God as follows: "Yes, when I work. When I am submissive and modest I feel somehow aided by *someone* who makes me do things which are beyond me. However I do not feel towards *him* any obligation because it is as if I were before a magician whose tricks I cannot see through. Consequently I feel deprived of the benefits of the experience which ought to have been the reward of my own effort. I am grateful without remorse." Barr says that Matisse's interest in the chapel "was artistic, not religious in any orthodox sense and he did not want his interest to be used for proselytizing purposes by the Catholics. On the other hand Matisse had not the remotest intention of allying himself with the Communists as Léger—and, far more conspicuously, Picasso—had done." In a statement of 1951 Matisse wrote: "In the chapel my chief aim was to balance a surface of light and color against a solid white wall covered with black drawings." Earlier he had approved a remark made by one of the monks: "Enfin, nous aurons une église gaie!"

With characteristic integrity, then, Matisse makes no claims for his art that it does not possess. He created in the chapel a moving ensemble of his essentially pagan art, perhaps a certain purification of that paganism, at least such a reduction of its sensual qualities to simplified terms that it could not give offense to any worshipper. But beyond that his faceless "St. Dominic," his schematized "Virgin and Child," his elongated bronze "Crucifixion" are as devoid of emotion as the cut-outs of *Jazz*. The door and window designs are almost pure abstraction. Only the "Stations of the Cross" indicate any intent to invest Catholic symbols with expressive intensity. It is said that Matisse studied Gruenewald's masterpiece when making studies for his "Crucifixion" but if he did there is no sign of it in the finished design. His "Stations" are bunched together as if it were his intention to throw them in the worshipper's face; they are rendered in a harsh shorthand, deliberately crude, with the effect of a

Matisse's Chapel at Vence. The disembodied saint, the stylized Crucifixion and the flowered windows combine to reflect the forms of religion rather than its content. *Below:* "Stations of the Cross." Were pictograms, drawn with deliberate crudity, the proper means of revitalizing the Passion for the penitent?

child's scribblings on a wall. The effect was of course intentional on the part of an artist who could draw as fluently as Rubens when he wanted to. But one wonders whether the "Stations" are legible to a communicant not letter-perfect in his devotional knowledge. (It is interesting to know that Matisse finally *numbered* them). And one doubts that anyone can take away from their contemplation any sense of human tragedy, drama or mystery.

Whether Matisse regarded such elements as hostile to art, or merely as having nothing to do with his own, there is no question that the critics who have given Formalism the inviolability of a religion looked with mistrust if not downright contempt on such an attitude. Since they cannot banish content from most of the arts of the past they commiserate with the Bruegels and de la Tours or praise them for painting good pictures in spite of this handicap. But when a contemporary is moved by a tragic sense of life—that is heresy. One of these critics, a painter who has spent a lifetime defending the Formalists against the conventional or the insensitive, recently took occasion in a review of MacKinley Helm's study of Orozco to state the formalist case against expressive content. In his urbane way he disposed of the great muralist by citing Élie Faure's disparaging remark that Mexican painting was no more than "something between Giotto and Michelangelo." Since it was archaistic, and since "a return to the past" was "obviously impossible," Orozco must be regarded as a personality rather than as an artist. Moreover he was to be condemned for giving—in such a work as his Prometheus bearing destructive fire to man—"a testimony on life and art" that was "negative." Orozco's "arraignment of conditions proposes no remedy for the evils he denounces." And among the real "revolutionaries" of art this critic mentioned—David and Cézanne.

David and Cézanne *were* revolutionaries, of course, but to insist that the revolution of form is the *only* revolution has become, as I shall try to establish in the next chapter, the last defence of a reactionary aestheticism. Only in times when artists lose every social or spiritual conviction does the frivolous notion that art's ultimate function is to define forms and arrange them in space, prevail. David was followed by Daumier, and Cézanne by Van Gogh. If in our century the tormented humanitarianism of a Munch, the compassionate indignation of a Rouault and the "negative" social affirmation of an Orozco will have served to remind us of more meaningful worlds that have been lost, then the art to come will be worthy of their spirit.

PART THREE

Epilogue:

The Eye of Man

Malevich's "Suprematist Elements" (*Collection Museum of Modern Art*). A 1913 drawing that reduced geometrical abstraction to its simplest terms but proved to be only the beginning of four decades of Formalism.

PART THREE

Epilogue:

The Eye of Man

The story is told of Cézanne that when one of his sitters fell off a chair, the irascible old painter shouted at him: "You're moving! The apples don't move!" True or not, the anecdote illustrates beautifully the modern artist's distaste for content, his drift first away from human interest to landscape and still life, then from still life to a cubist abstraction of a still life, and finally to the wholly non-objective picture. Cézanne found it much easier to evolve a pure construction out of apples, or a mountain, than he did out of a group of naked bathers, though he was ambitious enough to attempt the latter several times, and succeeded in making it almost as impersonal as his fruits and rocks.

Non-objectivism: Spartan and Profane

It was Picasso, however, taking his cue from Cézanne, who established both of the basic shapes that have determined today's abstract art. Out of his experiments with the presentation of objects seen from several angles at once, came geometric abstraction. As refined by Malevich, and later by Mondrian—whose elegant checkerboard canvases were often laid out in their final form after an exhausting elimination of less satisfactory arrangements with tape—geometric abstraction has enormously influenced the design of office-buildings, stage-sets, furniture and advertising layouts. In its seemingly endless varieties of color and texture, this limited art is still practiced by such American non-objective painters as Stuart Davis, Ralston Crawford, Fritz Glarner, George L. K. Morris, Ad Reinhardt, Joseph Albers and I. Rice Pereira. In England its most notable exponent is Ben Nicholson.[1]

Picasso himself tired of geometric abstraction before most of these

■

[1] Non-objectivism isn't confined to the English-speaking peoples, of course, but European contemporaries seem to shy away from the "pure" or "action" types, perhaps, it has been suggested, because World War II gave them their fill of regimented patterns and action. An exception is the French "Lyrical abstractionist" Georges Mathieu; see pages 137-8.

135

painters were old enough to wield a palette-knife. But the suggestive curves and amoeba-like "free forms" with which he immediately followed Cubism has provided incentive to this day for Non-objectivism's less Puritan contingent. These painters are the so-called biomorphic abstractionists. Their ancestors include Kandinsky, Matisse, Klee and Miró as well as Picasso. But their American progenitor was Arthur Dove, a contemporary of Marin and Hartley, who died in 1946. The late Arshile Gorky, Mark Rothko, William Baziotes, Adolph Gottlieb, James Brooks, Robert Motherwell, Charles Seliger, and to a certain extent the two most forceful American abstractionists, Jackson Pollock and Willem de Kooning, belong to this school.

It is perhaps unfair to describe the geometrist wing with the word "dull," but the rejection of so many of life's sensuous possibilities does tend to make such adjectives as "austere," "measured," "scholarly" and "pedantic" cross the mind. Davis' pictures, to be sure, are gay, with their clever arrangement of motives from urban life, and Pereira's, with her use of plastics and glass, are ingenious. Albers [2] and Reinhardt carry Malevich's Suprematist squares into rarefied realms of color harmony and dissonance. The late Bradley Walker Tomlin, in the words of Thomas Hess, found

Davis's "Midi." Geometrical abstraction derived from Picasso and Léger but owing its localized gaiety to such faintly recognizable ingredients of the American scene as factory windows, propellers and skywriting.

"elegance and taste at the roots of his inspiration" and tended "to make the whole action [of his pictures] one of embellishment alone." Nicholson's neatly tilted rectangles of color fall into place, Hess remarks, with an almost audible "click"—but so do the parts of precision-lathed machines whose functional adjustment is at least as satisfying to eye and ear.

That Gorky was well aware of his formalist antecedents is shown by the tributes he was famous for paying at dinner parties to Poussin and Ingres; but his paintings, like those of Miró and Klee, are enlivened not only by expressive uses of color, but by recognizable sexual motives and an engaging wit. His younger colleagues, though in general they are more

■

[2] The title of Albers' 1955 show was, appropriately, *Acting Colors*.

lyrical and talented than the geometricists, are almost as predictable. Gottlieb has compartmentalized the biomorphic and given it primitive antecedents. Baziotes has made it monumental and vaguely menacing. Seliger uses it as a matrix for fleetingly suggested natural forms. Rothko began by letting it flower poetically, then turned geometrist and arranged it in discrete pools of light. Pollock, the self-expressionist, squeezes it from the tube and flings it on the canvas as his unconscious commands. De Kooning's more complex approach with be discussed later on. A look at the intellectual pretensions of the Non-objective aesthetic is in order first.

Clive Bell and "Significant Form"

When Clive Bell's *Art* appeared in 1913, art criticism, in the English language at least, had pretty much confined itself to a scholarly apprecia-

Gorky's "Garden in Sochi" (*Museum of Modern Art*). Biomorphic abstraction at its most inspired, the beginning of a seemingly endless road populated with free forms, sexual grace notes and lumpy dragons.

tion of the arts of the past. Bell (and his friend Roger Fry, who had already written his famous *Essay in Aesthetics*) put an end to all that.

Bell began by asserting that the one quality common to every work of art—from a Persian bowl to a Cézanne—was "significant form" and that there is no way of recognizing such a quality except through "our feeling for it." His mention of Cézanne, and elsewhere in his book of Matisse and Picasso, who were not only also then virtually unknown outside of France but at the very thresholds of their careers, served notice that from now on the critics would call the turn, even for the avant-garde.

Bell's book was epoch-making in other respects. It established, once and for all, the assumptions of modern Formalism:

> The representative element in a work of art may or may not be harmful; always it is irrelevant. For to appreciate a work of art we need bring with us nothing from life, no knowledge of its ideas and affairs, no familiarity with its emotions . . . The pure mathematician rapt in his studies knows a state of mind which I take to be similar, if not identical.

Bell went on to contrast the "cold, white peaks of art" and its "austere emotions" with the vulgar attitude of the public, poking about blindly in "the snug foothills of warm humanity." Henceforth, not only the human should be eliminated from art, but all detail ("the fatty degeneration of art") and all informatory matter ("In a work of art nothing is relevant but what contributes to formal significance").

Looking back over the past, it is not surprising that Bell found the high points of European art in the Sixth Century Byzantine mosaics of Ravenna. In the Seventeenth Century, Poussin rather than Rembrandt or Rubens was naturally "the greatest painter of the age." ("You will notice that the human figure is a shape cut out of colored paper to be pinned on as the composition directs"—twenty years after Bell wrote this about Poussin, Matisse, as we have already observed, was to do exactly that.) As for poor Rembrandt, he was "a typical ruin of his age," losing his sense of form and design "in a mess of rhetoric, romance and chiaroscuro." Even Giotto, in Bell's canon, was hopelessly mired in content. ("He was always more interested in art than in St. Francis, but he did not always remember that St. Francis has nothing whatever to do with art.") Giotto was so "dreadfully obsessed," poor chap, "by the idea that the humanity of mother and child is the important thing about them." Cimabue "was incapable of such commonness." Was it not clear from this perspective that "since the Byzantine primitives, no artist in Europe has created forms of greater significance unless it be Cézanne?"

Bell was too sensitive and his honesty was too great to permit him to be wholly consistent. He could not help admitting that "the great ages of religion are commonly the great ages of art" or that all artists are essentially religious in the sense of being dedicated less to pleasure and things than to their beliefs and to capturing the image of an ultimate reality. He was forced, from this, to make a surprising admission. Next to the danger of being seduced by the problem of accurate representation, the greatest peril facing the modern artist, Bell asserted, was "the danger of aestheticism":

> The artist concentrates on making his picture "right." But most artists have got to canalize their emotions and concentrate on some more definite and more maniable problem than that of making something that shall be aesthetically "right." They need a problem that will become the focus of their vast emotions and vague energies, and when that problem is solved their work will be right.

Could Bell by any conceivable chance have been thinking of—content?

Bernard Berenson and "Tactile Values"

The outstanding art critic of the past half-century, Bernard Berenson, follows Bell in most respects, but, having a greater knowledge and experience of art, and being a philosophical humanist, his inconsistencies are more glaring. Since he began writing at a time when Ruskin and the Pre-Raphaelites had conditioned the public to think of painting entirely in terms of illustration, Berenson was naturally concerned to emphasize form—"tactile values" he called it. He was also inclined, for similar historical reasons, to go along with Croce and the Italian aestheticians in upholding the instinctiveness, spontaneity and even "irresponsibility" of the artist in the act of creation. "He [the artist] indulges in the free play of his gifts and has nothing else in his head . . ."

But Berenson, as already noted, was also a humanist. Conditioned perhaps by his childhood in peasant Lithuania and proletarian Boston, he could never quite rid himself of the nagging notion that a great artist should be a mouthpiece (even a popular mouthpiece) for great ideas. Could he have had Thoreau or Whitman in mind when he said that a poet must not only perceive the object but live it? The feeling that artists like Giotto, Raphael and Goya were popular not merely for meretricious reasons disturbed him. Perhaps, he said in one place, it was "because they created greater visual myths."

In his more guarded moments, however, Berenson is a typical spokesman for the age of Formalism. Art must be "intransitive," stimulating no desires or appetites. It must not be a cry from the heart. It must not traffic in indignation or pity or tears. Greco is ruled out for his "melodrama," and Bruegel and Bosch for their "mild nastiness." Giorgione and Titian, the great Venetian formalists, are "the Keats and Shakespeare of painting." And finally, unabashedly, comes the credo of Formalism itself:

> Real artists do not bother about feeling and vision, but only about learning how to draw and carve and paint in a more satisfactory way.[3]

Yet within two pages of this absurd statement Berenson contradicts himself! He admits that it is through content, *representational* content, and the artist's preoccupation with the spirit, that "the work of art fulfills its mission." And that it is "not the physical but the ethical, the moral weight" that overawes us in the presence of a Giotto, a Masaccio or a Piero della Francesca:

> Without spiritual significance the work of art may sink to the level of an object engaging the interest of the wine-taster or the curiosity of the antiquarian, and may rise at highest to the life-enhancing qualities of a spirited sketch, a Japanese *netsuke*, or a *danseuse* of Degas—mere playthings for grownups.

Is it surprising, in view of this deep ambiguity, that in his old age Berenson can still find a sympathetic outlet for his essentially academic aestheticism in the pages of *Art News*, the house-organ of American Non-objectivism, but that in Italy, where he chooses to live, he has become the relentless foe of every kind of a living art?

■

[3] *Aesthetics and History* by Bernard Berenson, New York, Pantheon, 1948.

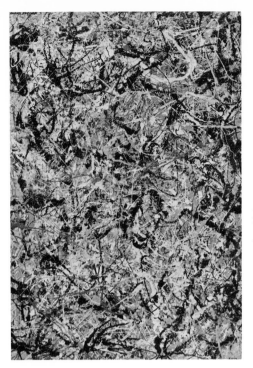

Pollock's "Number Eight." A critic provided the libretto: what it feels like to be inside a glass globe when the snow begins to fall.

Aestheticism Today: Greenberg and Hess

There are few such inconsistencies in the writings of Non-objectivism's latter-day oracles. Clement Greenberg and Thomas Hess have nothing but contempt for the introduction not merely of spiritual content but of any kind of content into art. Greenberg is sensitive, and perceptive enough at least when faced with content in the art of other ages, to sigh for lost grandeurs. But Hess, though he once admired the painting of Ben Shahn extravagantly, has no misgivings at all.

Greenberg's doubts are expressed in the article in which he examines his position most modestly.[4] He begins it with the axiomatic premise: Trust your instincts. Then, while admitting that all of us miss *something* in abstract work, he contends that most contemporary efforts to put image and object back into art result only in pastiche, parody or the pseudo-archaic. (The trouble could be, though Greenberg doesn't suggest it, that to paint image and object convincingly one must *feel* them, be sure of their relevance in a meaningful vision of life.) But Greenberg's next assumption is the trap. *He assumes that the only thing we miss in non-objective painting is the illusion of a three-dimensional world.* It never occurs to him that what we miss is the human, the emotional, the expressive, the spiritual. Then he himself gives one of the best imaginable critiques of Non-objectivism:

> Not only does the abstract picture seem to offer a narrower, more
> physical, and less imaginative kind of experience than the repre-

■

[4] *Abstract and Representational.* Ryerson Lecture at the School of Fine Arts, Yale University, May 12, 1954, printed in *Art Digest*, November 1, 1954.

Rothko's "Dark over Light Earth." The artist explained that he was painting pictures eight feet high because he wished to be enveloped by them.

sentational picture, but the language itself of painting appears, as it were, to do without nouns and transitive verbs, so that often we cannot distinguish centers of interest, etc.

But in the end, though Greenberg sounds a little desperate in his hope that art isn't in decline, that abstractionists will get better, or that their present pictures will become with familiarity more legible, he falls back on the formalist dogma. Connoisseurs of the future, he says wistfully, when they will look at the great representational pictures of the past

> may see the creation of an illusion of depth and volume as valuable primarily because it enabled the painter to organize such infinite subtleties of dark and light, of translucence and transparence, into instantaneous unity—into a decorative unity whose intricacies could not be controlled without the guiding notion of real three-dimensional objects familiar through practical experience.

Was the great realm of art ever given a more picayune definition? Well, if the future, like the present, is to comprise a society like our own in which artists and public are irreconcilably opposed, Greenberg is technically right. Otherwise the betraying word in his definition is "decorative."

Far from having any of Greenberg's weakness for the beguiling charms of representation in the arts of the past, Hess gathers the old masters into his fold. Being dead, they cannot protest. The feeling of satisfaction a spectator takes from an orderly Pieter de Hooch interior comes, Hess tells us, not "from any recognition of moral character or fidelity to historically ascertainable conditions, but from the fact that these forms and this paint are one and the same . . . This art of an orderly society is indeed for art's sake, for only then can it be for anyone's or anything's sake."

By isolating a fragment of a late Titian pastorale, Hess manages to make the further point that even the Venetian formalist's content is irrelevant: "The thin, sticky flecks and streaks of pigment weave into a surface which is never so much sky, tree, deer or hand, as it is an overwhelming affirmation of the existence of the artist's material." It follows from these examples, Hess continues, that what makes us enjoy a painting "has nothing to do with its species of subject, the accuracy with which this subject is represented, or the moral, political or subconscious motives of the artist." Indeed ". . . the appearance of, and resemblance to nature in a work of pictorial art can have nothing to do with its aesthetic value, except possibly, to act detrimentally."

Having made these content-defying premises, the rest of Hess's book,[5] his eulogy of the Non-objectivists, follows logically. Expressionism, in so far as it involves painting emotion-loaded objects or situations, as Van Gogh or Soutine did, is ruled out. It would be too risky. It would raise the possibility that the artist's sensations might fail to find corroboration in his craft. There is a safer way to paint pictures. ". . . In the tranquil but vehemently flaming landscapes of Matisse and Bonnard, the tortured duality of subject and object do not exist."

But Hess does not go for tranquility. He wants action,[6] *Sturm und Drang*, tragedy, even madness—so long as none of these is alluded to explicitly or given human referent. The answer is "to make the crisis itself the hero" of painting. This is what Hess credits de Kooning with doing, giving "pulse and motion to the unrecognizable" (whatever that may mean), endowing "the abstract form with tragedy or laughter, and on its own terms" (whatever *that* may mean). Having projected a symbol, as Hess calls it—de Kooning's "torn shape that dreams of humanity"—symbolism is admissible in action painting, but only if it refers to the act itself. Is such a gymnastic possible? "Symbols acquire added meaning" (Hess is here talking of Adolph Gottlieb's primitivistic pictographs) "from the increasingly complicated act that made them, *and they refer mainly to it.*" (My italics.) This, says Hess, is the place where Mondrian joins Soutine, and where Picasso can be left behind. The painter is not only painting the crisis; he *is* the crisis. Rothko makes his unadorned rectangles of light eight feet high because, as he himself explains, he makes "a more personal contact" with his work when it "envelopes" him. Pollock "urges the spectator to join in the paroxysm of creation." What it feels like to be communicated with by Pollock on these terms is described by Hess. "One feels," he says,

■

[5] *Abstract Painting* by Thomas B. Hess, New York, Viking Press, 1951.
[6] This term for the Pollock-de Kooning style of Non-objectivism originated in *Art News*, whose executive editor is Hess. In its pages, Lee Mullican, one of the Non-objectivists, is described as bringing to the attack "an uncontaminated frame of mind. . . . Form, color, composition, drawing can be dispensed with. What matters is the revelation contained in the act. . . ."

Mathieu painting "The Battle of Bouvines." For those whom the Nazis hadn't given their fill of "action": a dance of dedicated ferocity and the rejection of humanity.

"like the statuettes inside glass globes that, when shaken, are filled with snow flurries."

The Rejection of Man

In a recent article on Vorticism,[7] Geoffrey Wagner, the British novelist and art critic, quotes Wyndham Lewis, dean of the English avant-garde of the Twenties, as deploring the invasion of the sacrosanct artistic stage by the "dithyrambic spectator." Lewis saw this tendency as another fatal aspect of "democratic conceit," and his colleague Ezra Pound—who speaks of the arts as belonging to "a very few people" and of art as "a fluid moving above and over the minds of men"—agrees with him. Classical man, Wagner points out, enjoyed life and artistically idealized nature. The savage, on the other hand, according to Wilhelm Worringer, lives at odds with the natural world, and his art is an abstraction in the sense of a call to absolute values in a shifting and incomprehensible universe—and avoidance of life and a resentment of nature.[8]

Does the description apply to the artist in our time? It certainly appears to fit the Non-objectivists, at least as described and quoted in Hess's magazine. A reporter there describes the procedures and philosophy of one of them, the Frenchman Mathieu.[9] The two drove out one day to Bouvines,

■

[7] "Wyndham Lewis and the Vorticist Aesthetic" in *Journal of Aesthetics and Art Criticism*, September, 1954.

[8] Paraphrased from *Formprobleme der Gotik* by Wilhelm Worringer, Munich, 1912.

[9] "Mathieu Paints a Picture" by Michel Tapié de Céleynan, *Art News*, February, 1955.

the artist dressed up for the occasion as a Capet King (apparently to shock the peasants), his Rolls Royce loaded with General Staff maps and genealogical charts. Bouvines was the scene of a mediaeval battle and the "subject" of Mathieu's largest and emptiest non-objective painting. To paint it, the artist rented the Calmels studio on the Rue Marcadet where the biggest sets for Paris films are painted. Mathieu

> was dressed in black silk; he wore a white helmet, and shoes and greaves with white cross-bars. The film-maker, Robert Descharnes, shot the entire execution of the *Battle*. . . . in color to commemorate the event. And it was our good fortune to witness the most unpredictable of ballets, a dance of dedicated ferocity, the grave elaboration of a magic rite. . . .

Mathieu, the reporter adds, was

> paroxysmically conscious of the lofty duality of Monarchy-Anarchy . . . in an enormous and ferocious battle fought with cold steel in a struggle such as history perhaps will never again be able to stage . . . I think I can say that outside of certain paradoxical problems of logistics and long research and meditation on the culture of the Capetian monarchy, Mathieu regards everything as totally absurd and shows this constantly in his behavior, which is characterized by the most sovereign of dandyisms. He understands with complete lucidity all the dizzying propositions in the inexhaustible domain of the abstraction on which he has staked his whole life, every possible type of humanism having been rejected. . . .

Going beyond the field of painting, Worringer's statement applies to the Pound of the late *Cantos*, and equally to the poets and poet-critics who have followed in Pound's anti-humanist wake. Perhaps it also applies to Schoenberg and those composers who confuse physics with aesthetics by adhering dogmatically to a twelve-tone scale. That it does *not* apply to most modern poets and composers, I firmly believe. The content, the moral imperative if you will, of Frost and Eliot, Cummings and Sitwell, Eberhart and Auden, is patent. They want to communicate, they do communicate, and the measure of their communication is man. Though music is an expressive language that dispenses with intellectual concepts as such to convey feeling and character, the same can probably be said of Strawinsky and Britten, Sibelius and Berg, Copland and Menotti.

That Worringer's definition does not apply to most modern painters, including some of the Non-objectivists, I also believe.

But the danger that the definition is on the way to applying to *all* of us is real—and it is immediate. Only by applying himself consciously, and with humility, to the understanding of human and spiritual values can the artist of today and tomorrow function effectively in a world scarcely tolerant of his very existence.

The Limits of Realism

It is generally assumed that the antidote to extreme abstraction is realism. This is not necessarily so. We have already seen, at Forest Lawn, to what depths realism can sink. Academic realism represents just as much of a withdrawal from life as Non-objectivism. There is no greater aesthetic virtue in painting a table as the eye sees it than in so disguising its nature that its reality is lost; the thing is to paint a table in such a way that the spectator sees it, feels it and knows it for the first time, and in so apprehending it receives some insight into his relation to it and its relation to the world.

Berenson arraigns realism for not being "disinterested." It has a theology to defend. "It teaches that man is born a beast . . . that life is hell and that the only satisfaction to be got out of it is to recognize the fact and dance over it with a witch's sabbath of sneering glee." This is perilously close to Huntington Hartford's position. Its premise is a timorous aestheticism. Classicism, which idealizes, is not "disinterested" either, and certainly religious art is not if the artist—like the painter of the Villeneuve "Pietà"—projects supra-aesthetic values. Nevertheless, the degree of truth in Berenson's contention is in its application to that type of realism which does preach rather than express, which accumulates factual detail not for delight in the diversity of nature but to prove an intellectual point.

As already noted, most government-sponsored mural painting in the United States failed miserably because it merely enlarged an existing low-level realism, compounded of photography and caricature, to "prove" the political thesis that the American way of life depended upon the security of the Common Man. The thesis was "true" as far as it went. It was not ambitious enough. It was not humble enough. And the painters who discoursed about it on the walls of thousands of post-offices and court-houses did not believe in it deeply enough to paint its embodiment memorably. Content without supreme conviction never achieves convincing form.

Art Under Totalitarianism

Why, then, has not art under Nazism or Soviet Communism scaled the heights? Surely supreme conviction exists under such systems, at least in the minds of politically orthodox artists. But does it? It is in the very nature of art that the artist must be the final arbiter of what he creates. The Gothic master-builder believed in God, but one has to assume, after seeing what he produced, that he expressed that belief without duress and above all *without fear*. The forms he developed to express his belief evolved slowly over the centuries, not as a result of edicts from above but as a consequence of the painfully personal search of other free craftsmen in the tradition.

The important thing to be learned from a study of art under the dictatorships is not why a uniformity of sentimental mediocrity has been achieved—that was to be expected as soon as pervasive controls drove underground or within themselves all but those artists who were willing to provide (as Hollywood script writers do) the powers-that-be with the formulas they demanded. The important thing is to understand why foisting the shoddy art thus produced on the public aroused no resentment, and why in liberated Germany today, with all the controls removed, it is the Nazi painters and sculptors who are returning to favor—and even receiving official sanction.[10]

Art under Totalitarianism, I. Udo Wendel's "The Art Magazine." In Hitler's Germany: content without form —or taste.

The answer to the first question is that the dictators were quick to take advantage of the fact that artists and state were inalienably divorced. Even under the Weimar Republic, when the authorities had turned to the avant-garde for political posters and got nothing that the masses could understand, they called upon the academicians. Decades earlier William Morris had decried this unhealthy separation, insisting that "it is not possible to disassociate art from morality, politics, religion." Hitler, similarly denying the autonomy of art, saw that totalitarian integration would be impossible without control of spiritual needs, and proceeded to substitute the image of Nordic Man Rampant for the image of God in the hearts of the people—just as the Soviets had already done with their substitute, Working Class Man. They were able to get it accepted—and a dictator here would have no more trouble—because the abstractions of the avant-garde evoked no human or emotional response among the people, leaving a vacuum, an aesthetic yearning which even the unimaginative academician (there, as at Forest Lawn) was able to satisfy in some measure.

■

[10] See Hellmut Lehmann-Haupt's *Art Under a Dictatorship,* 1954. Emily Genauer, in an article in *The New York Herald Tribune,* more recently described "the relief" of tourists at the Venice Biennale when confronted with Iron Curtain illustration; these citizens of Topeka and Kalamazoo were so relieved by photographic realism that they could forget all about their anti-Communism! *This was their art.*

Dr. Lehmann-Haupt, a stanch defender of Non-objectivism, ridicules an article by the Soviet art commissar of Germany's Eastern Zone which had attacked formalism in art. ("An artistic entity," the commissar had written, "represents a firm union of content and form under the leadership of content.") Dr. Lehmann-Haupt also cites with distaste Hitler's statement that 95% of the national treasure of a people consists of its cultural achievements and only 5% of the "so-called material assets." But what does the good liberal offer in their place? Artists must preserve and cultivate their individualism. "Modern art is a powerful symbol of anti-totalitarian

Art under Totalitarianism, II. Gavril Miklossy's "Grivitza, 1933." When the Soviet satellites were given the green light to mass produce this kind of illustration, conservative Middle Westerners unwittingly applauded. (Compare Goya's "Executions of 3 May, 1808," page 70.)

belief." (See footnote on page 146.) Those who denounce modern art are the allies of political reactionaries. (This is the familiar guilt-by-association device.) People who look for an art contributing to America's (or democracy's) faith are misguided at best: "The artist is primarily concerned with his art, he has been, he still is, and he will be in time to come." But those who believe that artists like Goya, Daumier and Orozco were concerned with something greater than their art will not be satisfied with such conclusions; and those who believe that a working relationship between an artist and the society he lives in is one of democracy's critical and unfaced problems will be still less satisfied.

The Limits of Primitivism

Ever since Picasso borrowed from tribal sculptures to construct his "Demoiselles d'Avignon," primitive art has offered to many modern artists an inspiration if not a ready-made formula for avoiding the mercantile

Dubuffet's "Portrait of Joe Bousquet." The back-fence scrawls of vagrants and idiots momentarily invigorated a tired Expressionism, but could it say all about our world that needed to be said?

banalities of the Twentieth Century. Thus, to mention only the most powerful and distinguished of these talents, Giocometti has simulated archaic weathered bronzes in constructing his attenuated figures symbolizing the unattainable; Tamayo to some extent has objectified his fantasies of alienation in the terrifying idols of the Aztecs; Miró's painting is based upon a playfully Freudian interpretation of the art of children; and Dubuffet, rejecting the whole of Western art as debased by reason, knowledge and fashion, has made of the back-fence scrawls of vagrants and idiots an aesthetic principle.

That each of these, and many others looking backward, have produced works of authentic beauty there is no denying. The question is rather: to what extent has insight into the primitive mind contributed to an art fully expressive of our time? Has it not been too easy to suggest that we are all children and savages at heart, that the totems of children and savages say all about us that needs to be said?

Greenberg sees the wealth of orchestrated realistic detail in such early works as Miró's "The Farm" and "The Harlequin's Carnival" as concessions to sentiment. "Such lapses," he writes,[11] "were to be remedied as Miró progressed further toward the abstract." It could more truly be said that what Miró gains in formal harmony he loses in content value, and that as

■
[11] *Miró* by Clement Greenberg, Quadrangle Press, 1948.

he approximates the primitive shape he sacrifices human appeal. It is the same with Tamayo. The complexity and subtle nuances of color in this artist's present abstract phase hardly compensate for the loss of Mexico, a distinct place with recognizable peasant inhabitants that the artist, a Mexican and once a peasant himself, expressed unforgettably because it had been his life.

Magic-making, and the arts of early or isolated artists in the Western tradition, must not be confused. In the early centuries of Western art, the artist was a more accomplished artisan. He always had the skills, the decorative inventions, the tradition of anonymous craftsmanship to fall back upon between moments of inspiration. The conception of the Renaissance or post-Renaissance artist as an isolated Creator was undreamed of. Our nervous and often self-defeating compulsion to be different and unique did not exist. There was no need to deny content or abjure the communicative, because content was the common raw material of art and communication the object of the artist's language.

It is the same with the "popular" artist, the artist of today who happens to be out of contact with the formalist tradition. There is nothing "primitive" about Wilson Bigaud's "Mambo" unless the enlargement of the feet and hands be regarded as a want of skill rather than an instinctive distortion practiced for pictorially sound reasons in all monumental figure painting. As with Obin or Henri Rousseau, the self-taught painter in a community remote from the main currents of modernism takes his

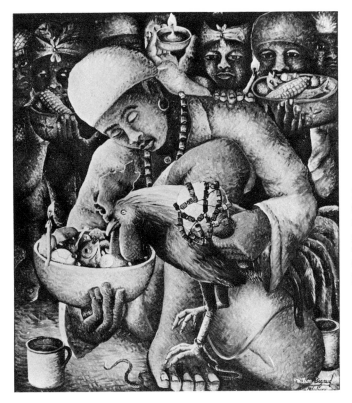

Bigaud's "Mambo." Revelation of what could be rediscovered intuitively of the grand manner by an artist who was at once an artisan of the people and a participator in their faith.

place with the more sophisticated masters of representation to the degree that his inventive or accidental stylistic shorthand enables him to approach the same destination of expressive content.

All primitives have one thing in common. Their art, no matter what form it takes, is busy with some world outside of itself. Whatever form best conveys that wonder, exorcizes that fear of the unknown, tells that heroic or human story—that form is the right one. The primitive never reproduces what has been made before. He has too much to say, and it is new. Nor does he imitate his contemporaries. There is no need for it. The more an artist strives for originality the less original he becomes. No two eyes see the same world; it is only eyes that focus on what other eyes have seen or done that do that. In the last analysis primitivism is a state of mind, a susceptibility to the miracles of the known world, rather than a backwardness in space or time. If today we find this state of mind more often on the fringes of civilization than at its centers, that is only because at the centers most artists have become too bemused by the burden of "art" to be bothered with the visible world or explore anew the inner one.

Beyond the Dream Image

Along with primitivism, the revelations of Freud and Jung seemed to offer to the artist a whole new world of symbolism and poetic imagery. To what extent has the modern painter made use of it?

Unlike the early Cubists and Futurists who glorified spatial dynamism and the machine, sometimes professing to see in the control of the latter the means of liberating mankind, the Surrealists expressed an anarchistic revolt of individuals against what they considered to be "the dead weight of a rational, technologically enslaved society." [12] Despite its promising beginnings in the wonderfully suggestive dream landscapes of de Chirico, Surrealism quickly degenerated into mystification and chic.

Only in the art of a few painters, like the Russian-born Tchelitchew and the Chilean-born Matta, both residents for long periods of Paris and New York, has Surrealism given any promise of becoming a serious art. Tchelitchew, with a virtuosity of line the equal of Dali's or Lebrun's, but with a disturbing sense of color, painted a number of large compositions in which nature, biologic growth and decay were so skilfully fused that they seemed to offer a synthesis of modern life. There was always something unpleasantly monstrous about these pictures, but then, hadn't Tchelitchew himself acknowledged this to be but a phase of his development? "I don't want to paint monsters," he told a poet. [13] "Pretty soon I will be tired of monsters. I want to communicate with people. That is painting. The ancients knew what painting was. It is to say something. It is to communicate." But unfortunately Tchelitchew became obsessed with the sinews and veins of his monsters, and finally with the configuration of their anatomy as mere lines of force. The Surrealist was on the way to becoming a Non-objectivist.

■

[12] *Abstract Painting and Sculpture* by Andrew Ritchie, New York, Museum of Modern Art, 1944.
[13] Quoted in *The Collected Essays of William Carlos Williams*, New York, Random House, 1954.

Matta's "The Thanksgiver." Modern worship of the machine and enslavement to its values provides an iconography of the sort that vitalized the arts of Dante, Brueghel and Bosch. *Below:* "To Cover the Earth with a New Dew." Satirical world of "The Thanksgiver" given depth and catharsis: biologic renewal and the poetry of new shapes and colors await the verdict of Man's power over Nature.

Matta's evolution, happily, seems to be in the other direction. Somebody has said that art which rids itself of pathos is a thing without consequence—just art with no other pretense. Matta by the power of symbol and suggestion has carried an art, that in its beginnings seemed little more than technicolor dreamscape, beyond this limitation. Since the War his canvases, without losing their jewel-like pools of light, have become battle-grounds on which is waged a symbolic war for the world. Constructing these pictures not from one fixed viewpoint but from several shifting ones, Matta involves us in a drama, the agony of today, a conflict of faceless, attenuated creatures with insect-like claws and knotted nerves. But at the same time there is a germination of new elements taking place under intense heats and lights, their forms and relationships vaguely apprehended: the rebirth of life. Thus, the ironically titled "The Thanks-Giver" shows man reduced to mechanism, surrounded by menacing shapes that resemble sun lamps, hair-dryers, typewriters, cash-registers, helicopters, bowing down stripped of his dignity before the idols of his own making. But in the even more powerful because less explicitly grotesque picture entitled "To Cover the Earth with a New Dew," there is suggested all the displacing of darkness and awakening of fresh beauty implied in the picture's title.

Asked by Emily Genauer [14] to explain the evolution of his work, Matta said that he had always painted effects, never specific images. "In the beginning he painted the beautiful rainbow world of his youth. Later came his realization of and horrified protest against human brutality. And now has come acceptance. Human beings are what they are, full of stresses and conflicts. But the world they live in is still beautiful—or can be, if men will reach out to identify themselves with each other. It is this constant reaching out, this needed interpenetration Matta is painting."

Matta disagreed with Robert Coates [15] who had called this vision "pessimistic." It is not pessimism, he told me later, but confusion out of which new things grow. "Our confusion, our perversion, is in thinking that we are better than other people. A family beefs about television; but do they smash their set? If they don't, and still beef, they're being snobs. A snob is one who pretends he's better than the masses, an intellectual idealist living in a world of double standards."

"The artist's function," he continued, "is to understand human relations. When religion was the center of things, we painted Christ or Buddha. Now we paint terrestrial—and public—relations."

Four Painters in Search of Reality

If anyone doubts that New York has displaced Paris as the painting center of the world, let him name four young French artists with styles as personal, as powerful and as ambitious as the four I am about to describe.

■

[14] *The New York Herald Tribune Book Review,* January 9, 1955.
[15] *The New Yorker,* January 15, 1955.

Moreover each of these four is fairly representative of a whole "family" of painters painting with somewhat similar intention, nor have I chosen in each instance the best-known representative of that family. My purpose here is merely to give specific proof of the variety of trails leading forward to expressive content and of the vitality of those blazing them through the undifferentiated formal forest.

(1) *De Kooning and the Emergent Human*

Willem de Kooning has been gently derided by some of the Non-objective painters with whom he is usually associated for trying to smuggle the image back into the "cleansed" picture. He certainly has not done so to achieve popularity. In fact, his dealer Sidney Janis tells me, any num-

De Kooning's "Woman IV." Would she find earthly antagonists? Would other figures follow—and in some kind of relationship to each other?

ber of de Koonings in the earlier non-representational style could find buyers today, and at four-figure prices. And, obviously, an approach to reality so tangential, so violent and so tragic in its implications as this later work, is no more acceptable to a likeness-loving public than was the "Crucifixion" series of Lebrun or the allegories of Beckmann.

Nothing but this artist's ability to master his environment (which relentlessly pushes him the other way) will decide whether de Kooning ultimately achieves that synthesis of significant content and form which characterizes great painting. As a boy in Holland he was apprenticed to a firm of decorators, and later he felt the full weight of the *Jugendstil* with its writhing biologic shapes. It would have been surprising indeed if he had not become a biomorphic Non-objectivist! Yet he has always managed to convey, somehow, even in his most abstract pictures, the sense of a human struggle between mortal contenders. As far back as 1951, in a statement made at the Museum of Modern Art (which Hess does not quote) de Kooning had said: "The argument often used . . . that painting could be like music and, for this reason, that you cannot paint a man leaning against a lamppost, is utterly ridiculous."

The same symptoms of a struggle to break out of the formalist strait jacket that we observed in Picasso's "Guernica" are present in de Kooning's latest works. The desire not to "finish" anything, to leave the frenzied initial sketch showing, to suggest anxiety by slashes of pigment in the unfashionable registers of mauve against crimson and olive green beside canary yellow may be in the heritage of subjective expressionism. But in the gat-toothed, cross-eyed grin, the clawlike hands and splayed heads, the spikey feet that have become the shoes they wear, the body ravaged as by a totalitarian torturer under a black sun, the struggle begins to assume human dimensions. Is it possible that de Kooning's development will be the reverse of Joyce's—from *Finnegans Wake* to *Ulysses* to *Dubliners*? That in his third phase, The Woman, the soliloquizing Mollie Bloom, will find earthly antagonists and even lovers? That instead of a figure, there will be figures—and in some kind of *relationship* to each other?

(2) *Perlin and Everyman's "Beauty"*

Bernard Perlin's almost photographically detailed paintings of familiar scenes would seem to have little relation to such Promethean ambiguity. They have in this sense. Perlin is one of a large number of contemporary American lyricists who are trying to see the world anew. Unlike de Kooning, however, these painters disclose a new vision of reality by starting with the familiar rather than the strange, with everyman's "beauty" rather than with the artist-anarchist's vision revealed professionally in the chemistry of paint itself.

Morris Graves, for example, paints a bird, a bowl, some rocks. The bird may be stripped to a haunting remnant of beak and eyes, the bowl to its glittering rim, the rock reduced to some terribly durable white lines scratched on black. The essence, the poetry, remains. The more ephemeral the bird becomes, the more its natural identity is manifested and its character as a

Perlin's "The Shore." Realism given validity again by restoring the world of remembered beauty to art through the intensity of the poet's imagination.

"critic" of man's pretensions sharpened. The more the bowl is simplified the more it acquires age and calls us to contemplation. Because the rocks, or Black Waves, are local they are universal.

David Fredenthal, taking his cue from those most American of formalists, Stella and Marin, will present a city as the sum of its cornices and bridges, its vehicles and its crowds; or a landscape as clouds, mountains and streams merging. Particularized, they can be unforgettable; but let the artist's conviction in this most dangerous kind of seeing relax for but an instant and the street can become a stage-set, the play of light as trivial as in a juke-box, and pathos sentiment.

Loren MacIver, still another venturer across this magical terrain, senses the temptations in her insistence upon the intimate and the familiar: "Quite simple things can lead to discovery," she says. "An ashcan suggests the phoenix; its relics begin a new life, like a tree in spring. . . . My wish is to make something permanent out of the transitory, by means at once dramatic and colloquial. Certain moments have the gift of revealing the past and foretelling the future. It is these moments that I hope to catch." [16]

Perlin avoids the trap by starting with the cliché itself—in his exhibition of 1955 the picture-postcards of tourist "musts" in Italy: the Coliseum, the Spanish Steps, Santa Maria del Salute, the Blue Grotto. It is a good starting point. Perlin says, in effect: the average man loves these romantic spots, but usually because he has been told to by a poet; he no longer looks at them; I will look at them so intensely that the magic for which they are justly famed will live again! And he does.

Asked by Emily Genauer whether painters like himself and William Congdon were attempting to distill meaning out of the most obvious, bromidic subjects as a reaction to content-less abstraction, Perlin replied: "Perhaps subconsciously. But with me it's because as I grow older, I realize that all the clichés we grew up rebelling against are true. The Coliseum at night is beautiful." Perlin implied that to crystallize remembered beauty and deepen the observer's perception of it was much more difficult than to paint

Bloom's "Cadaver II" (drawing). Modern man's shockingly new insight into his pitiful and defenseless mortality.

non-objective pictures. "It is a matter," the perceptive critic concluded, "of involvement with one's audience via the stimuli both share, as against detachment in order to experiment with purely technical problems."

∎

[16] Quoted in *Fourteen Americans* edited by Dorothy C. Miller, New York, The Museum of Modern Art, 1946.

Perlin's properties—the multifoliate fields, densely-figured walls and transparent pebbles—are tributes to Shahn, with whom Perlin worked during the War and whose happy marriage of style and reporting he admired greatly—but the poetry, the absolute pitch of his atmospheres and the arrested motion of his perfectly sculpted sleepwalkers, are his own.

(3) *Bloom and the Burning Bush*

Originating like Berenson and Shahn in the religiously saturated Jewish community of the Baltic States (he emigrated from Latvia to Boston at the age of seven), Hyman Bloom gravitated neither to the salons of Beacon Hill with their aura of aestheticism, nor to the revolutionary underworld of a class-conscious proletariat whose symbols could be drawn from the sidewalks, hiring halls and newspaper morgues. Introvert, mystic, moralist, and one of the great expressive artists of this age, Bloom takes his place in the company of Gruenewald, Van Gogh and Orozco by virtue of his capacity to feel within himself the most painful experiences of the human race and to personalize them in image and paint.

The pictures on which Bloom has been working for the past five years, a series of very large canvases of figures and *nature morte*, brazenly designed, dramatically presented and painted in lurid flame-reds and raw purples against a deliberately academic mat brown, have a certain resemblance to some of Lebrun's baroque slaughter-house and agricultural implement pictures of a decade ago. But technically they bear no resemblance at all to Bloom's earlier work with its Rembrandtesque portraits of patriarchs, its resplendence of detail and its low-keyed, luminous color. They seem rather to represent, as among the four artists who have affected Bloom most persistently, a turn to the defiant flesh-poems of Michelangelo and Blake as against the smouldering compassion of the early Rouault and the wild agonizing of Soutine. It is not a turn that puts to use Bloom's background and philosophic resources. For despite their subject matter, these gaudily fluorescent and arbitrarily simplified pictures seem to be a denial of both reality and death.

The "unpleasant" pictures for which Bloom is best known, the decomposing corpses and detached limbs of 1945–47, represent an entirely different approach—undramatic, spiritually involved and deeply moving. They were painted under the impact of the War and the extermination of the Jews, and while they may fail to communicate at first glance the love that is as much their emotional component as the revulsion, they may be interpreted as modern man's shockingly new insight into his pitiful and defenseless mortality:

> The beauty of the painting in a sense absorbs the subject matter into itself, and it is only then, when we have come to see the content through, and in terms of the painting, that its fullest and final meaning becomes clear. That meaning retains all our initial sensations of anguish, horror and pity at death, but it includes now

Bloom's "Older Jew with Torah." Like Rembrandt, this modern painter at his best presents a reconciliation of conflicting elements, a salvaging of the past and a translation of ritual into the heritage of the world.

what is also an exaltation and a triumph over death. Decay is transmuted into a living radiance, and the vital process, the endless mutation of matter, continues with a troubling beauty after death.[17]

The superficially "decorative" paintings of Christmas Trees and Chandeliers, images isolated from larger representational pictures which Bloom worked on during the War, have led Hess and some of the other Nonobjectivist critics to claim Bloom as their own—but with even less justification than in the case of de Kooning. While it is true, as Freedberg says, that this abstract phase, this translation of emotional sensation into vibrating light, may be regarded as "an extension to a logical extreme of a possibility inherent in one aspect of his style," neither symbol—the once life-bearing spruce, evanescently loaded with baubles of promise, and the inverted tree of light brandishing its daggers of glass so precariously over the heads of the disenchanted—is ever lost sight of.

The series of symbolic pictures that Bloom painted between 1943 and 1938, "The Synagogue," the "Child in the Garden," "The Jew with Torah" and "The Bride" (each in at least two versions) are more representational than the paintings just discussed but less so than the "Rabbi" of 1947—testifying to Bloom's habit of working on a number of pictures simultaneously, and to the homogeneity of his art. The second "Bride," less symbolic and more human than the first, is, as Freedberg points out, "a poetic seizing of the sensation of passage through an acutely poignant and meaningful moment of time. She is a web of feelings, images and memories that shift and shimmer within her as she wafts, transfixed and spiritualized, across the threshold of a new life . . . the painting *drawing its forms from the meaning it contains.*" (My italics.)

Being thus rooted in reality is the beginning, but only the beginning, of Bloom's secret. The "Child in the Garden" is actually based on a newspaper photograph of a child at an orphanage party; but its universality may be traced to its suggestion of the Christ Child and to the symbolism of baptism and rebirth indicated by the foreground pool. Its affirmation flows from the blazing foliage of spring in the background. Going back still further, "The Synagogue" of 1940, Bloom's first major picture, inevitably calls to mind Yeats' "Byzantium," and one is not surprised to learn that Bloom has been at various times a follower of Ouspensky, a Rosicrucian and believer in astrology. Like the poem, the picture is an extraordinarily rich reconciliation of conflicting elements, a salvaging of the past, a translation of ritual into the heritage of the world, and a hymn to origins.

(4) *Levine and Penelope's Web*

Except for the expressive intensity with which they apply paint, one would have little reason to think that Jack Levine and Bloom stepped into the world of art together. Their fathers were both immigrant shoemakers in

■
[17] *Hyman Bloom* by Sidney Freedberg, in Perspectives No. 6, Ford Foundation.

Boston. They were taken in hand as kids in the West End Community Center by a young art teacher named Harold Zimmerman, and later were given studios and stipends by Denman Ross, a collector and teacher at Harvard, who greatly helped Levine by revealing the technical secrets of the Old Masters and giving him respect for the conscious intelligence as a means of rivalling their mastery. It was Zimmerman (although Levine, unlike Bloom, was later to turn against his method of pursuing a succession of images to their source) who started both boys on the right track. Only nineteen himself at the time, Zimmerman had the good sense to encourage them in the mode of drawing they were already exploring—a street scene, a butcher's counter, a Chinese laundrywoman brandishing a flatiron, sketched without models from the memory. Levine says of this method today: "Drawing from models, from the object, leads to academicism or abstraction; you build up prowess against the time you'll have an idea; the other way, my way, you start with ideas and find the proper form in the process." [18]

Levine's studio, a high-ceilinged, dingy unpainted loft on West 12th Street, New York, has an appropriately opaque window facing the street: half of it is frosted like a lavatory glass and the rest is so dirty you cannot see out. The effect is as if to shut out the immediate presences of the people that crowd into Levine's mind's-eye so compulsively, and with them even the light. On the flap of a Moussorgsky album he showed me his credo. "To delineate the finer features of human nature and of the mass of mankind," the composer had written, "to penetrate resolutely into unexplored regions and to conquer them, that is the vision of the genuine artist." Levine himself, a gaunt, birdlike accuser, was working on a glowing but not exactly gay nightclub scene, and I asked him whether it was the "costume" of the place that attracted him. He said No; there had been a meeting of politicians there. "That was the beginning. That's my Sunday punch. I start there. But I'm ambivalent. I love satin robes, powdery faces, ruddy complexions, and they must come out too, though I hate that 'content'—or maybe *because* I hate it, who knows?"

In 1949–51 Levine did paint a number of semi-abstract pictures. "I was disturbed by the purism of the Non-objectivists," he told me. "For another thing, my own drive was weak then, and in consequence my content was becoming banal. I looked at my 'String Quartet,' which had become a popular success, and the more I looked at it the less I liked it. I began to 'measure' it, to see if the empty spaces couldn't be better accounted for, and so on. I even did pastiches of Rubens, Veronese, Titian. Then I measured some more. But finally I came to realize that all this wasn't necessary.

■

[18] I had been vaguely aware of this truth before talking with Levine, as a result of my experience with Bigaud in the St.-Trinité murals. Trying to determine why his figures were invariably *particular* people and at the same time Haitian archetypes, I had asked him whether he ever sketched from life. His answer was: "Never." On the contrary, his procedure was to go into his hut, close the door, turn on the naked overhead bulb and start drawing. The faces assumed archetypal reality because they emerged from a storehouse of memory deeper than the unassimilating porches of the eye.

The thing is to develop those things you have in your life. I went back to doing just that."

In the spring of 1953, while working on one of these new pictures, "The Gangster Funeral," Levine had put his thoughts in order—and on paper." [19]

He began by stating that man "is the legitimate and prior concern of

Levine's "Battle's End." Satire and poetry fused in allegorical painting of militarist covered with the confusion of self-awareness at the moment of his triumph. *Left:* Drawing by Levine.

[19] The quotations that follow are from Volume I, Number 1 of *Reality*. This paper, which Levine himself helped edit, grew out of an artists' manifesto reaffirming "the human qualities in painting" and deploring the trend to mere textural novelty then being encouraged "by a dominant group of museum officials, dealers and publicity men as the unique manifestation of the artistic intuition. This arbitrary exploitation of a single phase of painting encourages a contempt for the taste and intelligence of the public." The manifesto had been signed by most of the outstanding representational painters in the country, and even by such quasi-abstract artists as Karl Knaths, Robert Gwathmey, Abraham Rattner, Jacob Lawrence and William Thon. It was not signed by Shahn or Lebrun, Perlin or Bloom, Fredenthal or Andrew Wyeth. Perhaps because of this apparent division, and because it included a large number of the old-guard realists, its tone began to sound defensive and it failed to sway many of the younger artists committed to Formalism.

man" and that he himself had been led for stimulus and moral support to Masaccio, Rembrandt, Goya, Daumier, Van Gogh, Orozco and Rouault. "All considerations of modernity or contemporaneity as *criteria per se*," he added, "fill me with horror." Rejecting the dehumanization of the primitivists ("who climb back into the primordial ooze") and of the Non-objectivists ("Space Cadets . . . basing themselves firmly, although without much knowledge, on the higher sciences"), Levine asserted that the thing was not to go back to Rembrandt or to reject him "but to bring the great tradition with whatever is great about it, up to date." Then he described most frankly the considerations that went into the painting of the picture upon which he was then engaged:

> I should like to paint a narrative because it is possible for adolescents to buy marihuana and cocaine on our streets with the connivance of the powers-that-be. Consequently I am at work on a painting of a "Gangster Funeral."
>
> Immediately questions arise such as what sort of dress shall be worn. What do people wear at a gangster funeral? This may seem a concern for a dramatist, a novelist. I envy them these interesting concerns!
>
> If they be wearing street clothes instead of cutaways, it becomes possible to have the fat man show a broad mourning band on his thick little arm. It would be amusing to make it a heart instead of a band, but, unfortunately, that isn't possible.
>
> A widow. In deep mourning, clad in rich furs. Better yet, two widows! One very, very shapely.
>
> The chief of police, come to pay his last respects—a face at once porcine and acute—under no circumstances off to one side as a watcher. This would suggest a thesis other than mine, a policeman's thesis. He must be in the line of mourners, filing past to view for the last time the earthly remains of his old associate, who would, if he could, remonstrate with him for exposing himself in such a manner.
>
> If the chief's function is thus made clear, then it becomes possible to add a patrolman in a watchful capacity. I must now look for ways of establishing the identities of the mayor, the governor, *et alia*.
>
> It may be said that the idea is more fit for a novel or a film. This is ridiculous. As far as the novel is concerned, a picture is still worth a thousand words; as far as a film is concerned, the Hays Code requires it to show that crime does not pay, which is not my thesis either.
>
> This libretto in no way invalidates the possible creation of a work of art. On the contrary, it inflects it, it enriches it, it makes the project more complex. I see no harm in putting the conscious mind to work in this fashion.
>
> Today movement toward disintegration is considered developmental. The artist is considered to be casting off academic fet-

ters. As though Penelope, unweaving at night what she wove by day, liberated herself by so doing!

This is the side-to-side movement of an involuted craft. It could be said that somewhere there is a golden mean—a critical moment in the weavings and unravellings of Penelope—that would be the moment in which all the art I love has been created.

The names I celebrate are those of the dramatists.

Levine's "Gangster Funeral." Artist's conscious effort to discard obscure symbolisms and renew himself upon the visible aspects of whatever seems most meaningful in his time.

Perlin, whom I encountered one day in a joint retrospective exhibit of Levine and Bloom at the Whitney Museum, stopped in front of one of these flickering sermons of Levine, contemplating it for some time. "Both are sublime painters," he said, "but when Levine tries to emulate Rembrandt, the tenderness that creeps into his smaller pictures perhaps despite his intention, is missing. Bloom, on the other hand, succeeds in painting precisely like Rembrandt without trying to at all—but only in those earlier pictures that embody his love affair with life." It was a good point, though

Lawrence's
"Barber Shop."

it failed to account for Levine's more steady growth and diversity. The excess of hatred, of the will to punish, may be a limitation in Levine, but his conscious effort to do away with obscure symbolisms and renew himself upon the visible aspects of whatever seems to him most meaningful in his time is an enormous asset. He is just as much opposed to the "subjective arrogance" of Expressionism, he says, as he is to the dehumanization of the Non-objectivists. "Individuality at the expense of communicativeness is not finding oneself, it is losing oneself. I have always distorted for satire or pathos or one thing or another, but never just to express myself."

Lloyd Goodrich points out [20] that social comment and satire didn't enter painting of the American scene until the WPA projects of the Thirties, on which almost all the painters discussed here, including Graves, Shahn, Lebrun, Bloom and de Kooning, worked at one time or another. Nineteenth Century American artists like Mount, Bingham and Homer concentrated on the cheerful side of common life. Later on, Henri, Sloan, Marsh and Hopper treated America as a spectacle—exuberantly or meditatively, according to their temperaments. Even Jacob Lawrence, who shares with Shahn and Levine the capacity of making us see what is under our noses as we never did with our own eyes, is basically a story-teller, cutting through with Orozco-like simplifications to the absolute visual essence of what goes on in a pool hall, a shooting gallery, a barber shop or a coal mine, but no further. Levine tells stories too, but he succeeds in making myths or monuments of them. At his worst he can be sentimental, cruel or fulsomely romantic. But at his best, because he is willing to take these chances, he restores to modern art the grand manner: purposeful content that creates its own forms.

■

[20] In the Foreword by Frederick S. Wight to a catalogue of Jack Levine's work printed by the Institute of Contemporary Art, Boston, 1953.

The Artist and Society

Nothing more clearly dramatized the crossroads at which art stands today than a controversy arising out of the most popular exhibition ever mounted by the Museum of Modern Art. This exhibition was the 500 photographs assembled in 1955 by Edward Steichen from over 2,500,000 prints submitted by professionals and amateurs in sixty-eight countries and entitled "The Family of Man." The tremendous emotional impact on the public of these insights into man's moods from birth to death became the occasion for an article by one of Non-objectivism's most persuasive champions.[21] Aline Saarinen raised the question whether photography hadn't "replaced painting as the great visual art form of our time." She went on to argue that to photography ("a folk art") now belongs the business of supplying the public with "immediately intelligible" and "universal" statements of "easily assimilable emotional impact." Had not painting, Mrs. Saarinen asked, "become so introverted, so personal, so intellectualized that it has lost both its emotion and its power of communication?" Painters, she concluded, "should now be reinforced in their conviction that they have no *responsibility* toward depicting the outward appearance of the world or even finding 'the hidden significance in a given text.'"

Ben Shahn's letter taking issue with this limitation of the painter's role began by noting the public's obvious craving for expressive content, a craving now ironically shared by Mrs. Saarinen herself—"even though the exhibition stood in exultant contradiction to every precious principle which she and the majority of art writers have laboriously hung about the neck of art across a decade of literary effort." Shahn asked why the painter must be denied the inspiration of outward appearances? "Must one reject Praxiteles in order to appreciate Noguchi?" Was there any area in the world that was not the proper preserve of *both* the painter and the photographer, provided either one was able to make of it a great symbol? As for the danger of the painter dealing in "too easily assimilable" materials:

> A few days ago *The Times* reproduced a painting by El Greco showing the body of Christ received in the arms of Mary. The meaning of the work is so easily assimilable that not even a single line of art comment is required for full comprehension. Is El Greco, then, a folk artist?
>
> The reviewer, it seems to me, presses upon the artist a *responsibility* more onerous than any he has ever yet had to bear—namely the warning that responsibility may not be for him. Has it ever occurred to Mrs. Saarinen that perhaps the artist *wants* to be responsible? Is he not human? Does he not share the great common experiences of man? Has he not witnessed death and tragedy and birth? And is he, by some grievous miracle, exempt from the ordinary human reactions to such experience?

■

---

[21] "The Camera vs. The Artist," by Aline B. Saarinen, *The New York Times,* February 6, 1955. Ben Shahn's letter of reply, quoted in the following paragraph, was printed in the same paper the following Sunday.

Shahn stated his personal conviction that the status of painting as an art was a higher one than that of photography, not because the one was responsible and the other irresponsible, but because painting was able to contain a richer expression of the artist's own capacities. Then he concluded:

> Let us also note that it is not at all surprising that the public turns to the Steichen show with such undivided enthusiasm. The reason is, I am sure, that the public is impatient for some exercise of its faculties; it is hungry for thinking, for feeling, for real experience; it is eager for some new philosophical outlook, for new kinds of truth; it wants contact with live minds; it wants to feel compassion; it wants to grow emotionally and intellectually; it wants to live. In past times all this has been largely the function of art. If art today repudiates this role, can we wonder that the public turns to photography; and particularly to this vivid show of photographs that have, it seems, *trespassed* into almost every area of experience?

Even the creator of communicative intent who earnestly tries to be fully responsible to the public is finding it hard to "trespass." How hard, is shown by the recent experiences of some of the artists discussed in the Prologue to this book. It will be recalled that Bernard Rosenthal's "Crucifixion" of 1951 was one of the modern works that—despite its religious subject matter—drew from the Los Angeles City Council intemperate charges of subversion. In 1955, when the same artist's semi-abstract and faceless "American Family" was unveiled on the façade of the Police Facilities Building, the same civic body called for the removal or destruction of the new work. Because these bronze figures had been commissioned and approved in advance of their unveiling, local artists once more united in defense of freedom of expression—rightly and successfully. This time, however, considering the location of the work and its permanency, the question of the *public's* rights deserved more thought than it got. If art in public places, like Rosenthal's—and even more so in the case of such really irrelevant public statements as Léger's blown-up doodles in the United Nations General Assembly Building in New York—fails to communicate in human terms, are the human beings that must live with it day in and day out justified in desiring to replace it with an art that does? It is a difficult question. The artist's sense of responsibility must always be a personal thing,

Rosenthal's "Family Group." Its appearance on a public wall raised the question whether the artist's responsibility extends beyond the work of art when he moves into the marketplace.

and its value for the public lies in the supposition that the public ultimately may rise to that personal truth which the artist has discovered. Surely the public will *not* rise if the artist refuses to respond to life, makes no effort to comprehend the world he lives in, or fails in that communication of emotion which is at the foundation of all art.

But granting that formalistic monologues conducted in the marketplace only serve to widen the gap between artist and public, is the marketplace the proper forum today for even the artist whose passion is to communicate what he has to say about Man, Nature and God? Has the easel picture become so exclusively a symbolic vehicle of subjectivism and high-priced scarcity that its very frame predetermines privacy? Are the Non-objective painters themselves making larger and larger pictures because of an unconsciously growing distaste for the intimacies of hermetic expression; and are the Motherwells and Gottliebs, like Matisse, accepting commissions from religious institutions because even a meaningful *setting* gives a communicative dimension to an uncommunicative image? Does governmental insensitivity to all but illustrative propaganda these days doom the serious artist to dependence on a small group of wealthy collectors? Can the artist, under these circumstances, ever recover the status of a public servant and conscience he held in the days when he was an artisan and a collaborator in society's grandest undertakings?

Ultimately—unless he is resigned to being a social and economic parasite—the artist's salvation must lie in what he can accomplish as a functioning member of the community he lives in. But unless the will to integrate his activities with society's and be a spokesman for its highest values is his own, no public activity on his part will bear living fruit. There are many possible paths to the recovery of such a relationship. One may be through industrial design, a field in which modern artists have already made major creative contributions. Another could be in such increasingly popular media as the lithograph, the colored woodblock and the silk-screen print by means of which whole schools of inventive contemporary craftsmen working through such organizations as the International Graphic Arts Society are now extending the frontiers of art into the middle-class home. But if the highroad lies on walls, or crosses public places, then artists who have something to say will have to wait until they are in a position to dictate their own terms as they have in the past. Ways will have to be found of raising the public sights to an enjoyment of an art of expressive content rather than lowering the artist's standards or merely imposing his taste on an indifferent or unwilling public. The re-education of governmental officials to an appreciation of the rewards of art has not even begun. The new artist may have to start painting murals, if the mural is to be his medium, in schools, churches, offices, stores, homes—even his own home.

Making formalist decorations for public places, like Matisse, Léger, Rosenthal, is not to be confused with this kind of an art of "engagement." An art inherently communicative is today just as far from having a receptive audience as any other. In fact today the pressure on the artist of expressive content to retire into the shell of privacy is even *greater* than the pressure on the formalist. After all, people may laugh or shake their heads at a surface covered with straight lines or squiggles but they can hardly be offended; is there anything by its very nature less controversial than an arabesque? What the moralist has to say about the world we live in, on the other hand, is almost certain to disturb the complacent and infuriate the guilty.

We have seen how Lebrun was compelled, in his rejection of the banal script offered by Tulsa, to fall back on a spiritual content of his own choosing in a mural without walls; society's indifference to that project and its impugning of his motives has now, it appears, driven Lebrun back upon defiant abstraction. It may be significant, too, that the only mural commission Shahn has been offered since his New Deal projects of the Thirties—a decoration for a shopping center—could be fulfilled only in his least expressive idiom, a repetitive pattern of wire package-carriers approaching geometrical abstraction. Even this formula, in the end, was rejected as "too modern." The road ahead for the artist of expressive content is going to be a rough one, and if he wants to find allies he may have to wander much further than he is now willing from the strictly patrolled one-way street of Non-objectivism.

The Mind Considered as a Sixth Sense

A critic in *Art News* insists that "The only thing that counts for modern art is that a work shall be new." Franz Kline, a Non-objectivist painter quoted in the same publication, takes the idea a step further. "The emotional results count," he says, "not intellectual afterthoughts." But Louis Danz, another spokesman for the Non-objectivist aesthetic, carries this train of thought to its logical conclusion: "The artist must deny the very existence of mind." [22]

Is this the kind of thinking Picasso was referring to when, in the foreword to his most recent work, the series of drawings entitled "The Human Comedy," he struck out against artists who are "not sensuous and who become intellectual but not intelligent"? I think so. He may even have had the inhumanity of his own earlier, but not earliest, styles in mind. Certainly the new drawings—with their theme of a scrawny, fashion-weary intellectual confronting an ideally beautiful but mindless woman—are human and humorous as well as sensuous, and abundantly communicative too.

But the temptation to forego intelligence by retreating into the cozy caverns of the mind is not, as we have seen, new. The composer Gluck recognized it toward the end of the convention-ridden Eighteenth Century when he said that the music of opera must return to the words. Today we are mortally afraid of words (nature, meaning, moral definition) and especially of how our words may be interpreted. The great physicist, Robert J. Oppenheimer, who had plenty of reason to repent his outspokenness and the rash injection of human considerations into a logistic equation, warns artists that they may have to retreat into the universities. With traditions, symbols, myths and common experience dissolved in a changing world, the

■

[22] *Dynamic Dissonance in Nature and the Arts* by Louis Danz, New York, Farrar, Straus & Young, 1952.

university, Oppenheimer says, "will protect him from the tyranny of man's communication and professional promotion."

But will it? Oppenheimer admits elsewhere that the artist must somehow become part of the community in order to illuminate "the great and terrible barrenness in the lives of men." This is true for society's sake, but also for the artist's. The poet Edith Sitwell, it has been pointed out, made her reputation in the Twenties and Thirties writing a "tense, inspired and highly sophisticated doggerel" characteristic of modern formalist verse. But she became a great poet, under the impact of the War's human suffering and waste, when to her technical virtuosity she added "the moral earnestness that makes English poetry great." [23]

Formalists, seeking philosophic justification for their retreat to the sanction of the senses alone, have been known to cite Hume's famous definition: "Reason is, and ought only to be, the slave of the passions." What Hume actually meant has been translated into our terminology by Bertrand Russell: Reason cannot supply the ends, but only reason can choose the right means to the end. Now let us apply this basic truth to aesthetics. Reduced to its simplest equation:

Reason without Intuition = Academicism
Intuition without Reason = Formalism
Intuition *plus* Reason   = Expressive Content

Those who in the name of the emotional life wish to limit the rule of reason are in fact, Russell shows, only asking that man's emotional life be frustrated.

Everyman's Art

To make a final point, let me turn to that art which is considered in its very nature the most "abstract," [24] and to the work of an artist the greatness of whose creation is not likely to be questioned:

> It is generally admitted that Beethoven's Fifth Symphony is the most sublime noise that has ever penetrated into the ear of man. All sorts and conditions are satisfied by it. Whether you are like Mrs. Munt and tap surreptitiously when the tunes come—of course so as not to disturb the others—or like Helen, who can see heroes and shipwrecks in the music's flood; or like Margaret, who can only see the music; or like Tibby, who is profoundly versed in counterpoint and holds the full score open on his knee; or like their cousin, Fräulein Mosebach, who remembers all the time that Beethoven is "echt Deutsch"; or like Fräulein Mose-

■

[23] Quoted from a review by the modern poet Kenneth Rexroth in *The New York Times*, January, 1955.

[24] Like all the arts, music may or may not be formalist, but the attempt to equate it with mathematics, rather than with poetry or painting, is ridiculous. Beethoven was so un-mathematically inclined that to get the product of 5 times 17 he had to write 17 out 5 times and reach the result by addition.

Matisse's "Christ on the Cross." Religious art de-humanized in a world mortally afraid of "words."

bach's young man, who can remember nothing but Fraülein Mosebach; in any case, the passion of your life becomes more vivid, and you are bound to admit that such a noise is cheap at two shillings.[25]

What is the secret of this universally communicative emotional content in Beethoven's music? It is now known, though romantic biographers have tried for a century to conceal it, that Beethoven was a maladjusted human being, psychically and physically; that he could not get along with other people; that he failed to understand himself; that he had no control over his temper; that he cheated his publishers, beat his servants, humiliated his friends and drove his nephew to attempted suicide. Certainly, the formalist will say, here is proof enough that his art can be no reflection of that life or those morals! Yet it is! In addition to all these unpleasant social characteristics, Beethoven had (it is equally well known) an immense capacity for love. He felt affection and pity as well as anxiety and aggression. He could be generous and outgoing, self-critical as well as condescending; loyal as well as spiteful; unforgiving one moment and remorse-

■

[25] *Howard's End* by E. M. Forster, New York, Alfred Knopf, 1943.

ful the next; childishly rebellious, materialistically grasping, and at the same time maternally solicitous or indifferent to everything but the benign compassion of God.

The *content* of his music, what makes it everything Forster says it is and more, is in the fact that it expresses with heroic honesty these conflicts—and resolves them, as Beethoven in his life never could. There are absolutely *no inhibitions* to their expression in the music, no formalistic tricks—and therefore no barrier between the artist and his equally fallible audience. *How* these conflicts are resolved we cannot understand, nor need we—that is the measure of the composer's genius. But to participate, beyond understanding, in their courageous resolution, is to experience art on the highest level, the level inhabited by painters like Giotto, Michelangelo, Greco, Rembrandt, Daumier and Orozco, and in their great moments by such as Van Gogh, Rouault, Shahn, Levine and Bloom—the level at which art's two faces become one.

Shahn's "Incubus." Spiritual expression out of involvement in the web of secular life. The level at which art's two faces once more become united.

ACKNOWLEDGMENTS

While the thesis of this book may seem to owe a good deal to the three authors quoted most frequently in its pages—Professors Arnold Hauser and David Robb, and André Malraux—I have no reason to anticipate that any one of them, whose books I read for the first time in 1953, would subscribe to it. Their creative scholarship and insights did, however, serve to confirm views expressed in a variety of ways over the past two decades. Readers of any of the five anthologies of poetry I edited between 1938 and 1949 will be familiar with those views. Readers of any of my three previous books about artists—especially *Portrait of the Artist as an American*—will be aware of the specific application of those views to painting.

Actually the genesis of this book dates back further. In 1931, following graduation from college, I went to Italy to write a book about Piero della Francesca. I didn't write it. Already the *why* of art seemed to me at least as important as the *how*, and since clues to the mysterious content of the great muralist's work proved elusive, I turned elsewhere. Still further back, the first piece of critical prose I can remember attempting was a schoolboy essay on the connections between Leonardo da Vinci's life and his art. (Later, in 1941, I tried in *The Airmen* to make *poetic* sense out of that enigma.)

The first intimation of the present book as such took place during a trip to California in the fall of 1951. My intention then had been to write a study of the evolution of Rico Lebrun's "Crucifixion" series. It was to be published by the University of California Press. To that house, and to its director, August Frugé, I owe a debt of gratitude for encouragement, generosity and forebearance. In consequence of the artist's modesty and the author's conviction that some revelation of an expressive artist's life is required for a full understanding of his art, the monograph little by little turned into the present very different book. Nothing of the original study has appeared so far, save an article in *Perspectives USA*, published by the Ford Foundation, and the few pages concluding the Prologue here. Another passage in the Prologue, the description of Simon Radilla's towers in Watts, was to have been a part of an earlier version of this book; in extended form it was printed in 1952 by *New World Writing No. 2* under the title "The Artist Nobody Knows." I acknowledged the help of Jules Langsner then, and it is a pleasure to do so again. Other friends in California who were most helpful should be mentioned. These include my father-in-law, Colonel Z. Wojciechowski, and his wife and their sons, with whom I lived in

Hollywood for several months with my family; and Sisters Carita and Magdalen Mary of the Art Department of Immaculate Heart College, who gave, and continue to give me, hope that the Church may once again call upon the full resources of a living art, conferring upon the artist in return the inspiration of a content greater than his subjective resourcefulness. This hope had been stirred in me two years earlier by Bishop Alfred Voegeli, while I was in Haiti directing the mural work of the primitive painters in his Cathedral St.-Trinité.

For reading the manuscript and offering invaluable suggestions as to details I would like to thank Ben Shahn, Alexander Eliot, Alastair Reid, T. O'Conor Sloane III, and my wife, Maia. George Thompson, who designed this book as well as my *Haiti: The Black Republic,* deserves to be thanked doubly. To Joseph Grippi, whose Gallery G in New York provided a brief haven for the Haitian artists, and more recently an oasis for the kind of painting and sculpture we both believe in, I express my appreciation. To such dynamic younger artists as Meyer Lieberman, James J. Kearns, Leonard Baskin, Ugo Frasconi, Joseph Glasko and André Racz I submit this note of regret: familiarity with much work confirming my hopes for art came too late to permit tribute in the text.

ILLUSTRATIONS

The Eye of God. Detail from Obin's mural in the Cathedral St.-Trinité, Port-au-Prince, Haiti, showing adjacent mural by Rigaud Benoit. Photo: Byron Coroneos.

Original pencil sketch for Obin's mural. 1950. Collection the Author.

Cherubs and Children, 1946. Ben Shahn. Collection Whitney Museum of American Art, New York.

Aimee Semple McPherson. Press Photo.

Christ in Hollywood, 1952. Oscar de Mejo. Courtesy the Artist.

Mystery of Life group (detail). Professor Ernesto Gazzeri. Forest Lawn Memorial Park. Photograph by the Author.

Crucifixion (detail), c. 1898. Jan Styka. Forest Lawn Memorial Park.

Crucifixion Set from Darryl Zanuck's Cinemascope "Jerusalem." 1952.

The towers of Simon Radilla. Watts, California.

Details from Radilla's towers. Photos by the Author.

Huntington Hartford with examples of "good" and "bad" art. Courtesy *Life*.

Rico Lebrun working on a panel of the "Crucifixion" triptych. Photograph by Ann Rosener.

Burning Spinner. 1950–51. Rico Lebrun. Collection Agnes Moorehead, Los Angeles, California.

Beggar with Crutches. Trial lithograph for a series executed at Colorado Springs, c. 1944. Rico Lebrun.

Crying Machine. Pen drawing by Rico Lebrun. 1948. Collection the Author.

Soldier on Arm of Cross. Drawing by Rico Lebrun, 1950. Collection the Artist.

Crucifixion Triptych. Rico Lebrun. 1952. Collection the Artist.

Two Prostitutes. 1906. Rouault. Watercolor and pastel. Collection Dr. and Mrs. Harry Bakwin, New York. Photograph by Siochi Sunami, Museum of Modern Art.

Head of Christ. Byzantine Mosaic. Sixth Century. Ravenna.

Portrait of Kahnweiler, 1910. Picasso. Collection Mrs. Gilbert W. Chapman, New York.

Portrait Head, 1948. Joseph Scharl. Courtesy Gallery St. Etienne, New York.

Stained Glass Façade, Milton Steinberg House, New York, 1954. Painter and designer, Adolph Gottlieb. Architects, Kelly and Gruzen in association with S. Robert Greenstein.

Sculptured figures from the Autun Tympanum. Twelfth Century.

Villeneuve (Avignon) Pietà. Fifteenth Century. Louvre, Paris.

Pietà Fresco in the Arena Chapel, Padua, c. 1305. Giotto.

The Vision of St. Eustace, c. 1425. Pisanello. National Gallery, London.

Holy Trinity, c. 1428. Masaccio. Fresco in Santa Maria Novella, Florence.

Battle of Naked Men, c. 1475. Engraving by Antonio Pollaiuolo. National Gallery of Art, Washington, D.C.

Resurrection, c. 1465. Fresco by Piero della Francesca, Borgo San Sepolcro.

Flagellation, c. 1475. Piero della Francesca. Urbino.

Sacred and Profane Love, 1512. Titian. Borghese Gallery, Rome.

The Last Judgment (detail), 1535–40. Fresco by Michelangelo in the Sixtine Chapel, Rome.

Crucifixion (detail), 1565. Tintoretto. Scuola San Rocco, Venice.

Crucifixion (detail), c. 1512. Gruenewald. Colmar, Germany.

Christ Bearing His Cross, c. 1505. Bosch. Kunsthistorisches Museum, Vienna.

Temptation of St. Anthony (detail), c. 1512. Gruenewald. Colmar.

Resurrection (detail), c. 1512. Gruenewald. Colmar.

Resurrection, c. 1596. El Greco. Prado, Madrid.

View of Toledo in a Storm, c. 1614. El Greco. Metropolitan Museum, New York.

Return of the Prodigal Son (detail), c. 1665. Rembrandt. The Hermitage, Leningrad.

Old Woman Cutting Her Nails, 1648. Rembrandt. Metropolitan Museum, New York.

Descent from the Cross, 1653. Rembrandt. National Gallery, Washington, D.C.

Three Crosses, 1653. Etching by Rembrandt. National Gallery, Washington, D.C.

Triumph of Neptune and Amphitrite, 1639. Poussin. Philadelphia Museum of Art.

Lictors Bringing to Brutus the Bodies of His Sons (detail), 1789. David. Louvre, Paris.

Why? Etching and Aquatint from "The Disasters of War" by Goya. c. 1805.

Executions of the Third of May, 1808. 1814. Goya. Prado, Madrid.

Job's Despair. Water-color by Blake, c. 1825. Pierpont Morgan Library, New York.

Grande Odalisque, 1814. Ingres. Louvre, Paris.

Scenes of the Massacre of Scio, 1824. Delacroix. Louvre, Paris.

The Woman with a Parrot, 1866. Courbet. Metropolitan Museum, New York.

Rue Transnonain, 15 April 1834. Lithograph by Daumier.

Don Quixote and Sancho Panza, c. 1865–70. Daumier. Collection Mr. & Mrs. Charles S. Payson, New York.

Déjeuner sur l'Herbe, 1863. Manet. Louvre, Paris.

La Grande Jatte, 1886. Seurat. Art Institute of Chicago.

The Bathers, c. 1898. Cézanne. Philadelphia Museum of Art.

The Potato Eaters, 1885. Van Gogh. Collection V. W. Van Gogh, Amsterdam. Photo Soichi Sunami, Museum of Modern Art.

At Eternity's Gate, 1882. Lithograph. Van Gogh. Private Collection, New York.

Night Café, 1888. Van Gogh. Collection Stephen C. Clark. Photo by Soichi Sunami, Museum of Modern Art.

The Yellow Christ, 1889. Gauguin. Albright Art Gallery, Buffalo.

Red Haired Woman, 1908. Rouault. Courtesy Knoedler Gallery, New York.

Portrait of Mr. X, 1911. Rouault. Albright Art Gallery, Buffalo, N.Y.

It is you, my Lord, I recognize you. Etching from Miserere et Guerre, 1927. Rouault. Collection Museum of Modern Art.

The Old King, 1916–36. Rouault. Carnegie Institute, Pittsburgh.

Maternity, 1941. Soutine. Collection M. et Mme. Marcellin Castaing, Paris.

Jealousy. Munch. Lithograph, 1896. Collection Museum of Modern Art.

Entry of Christ into Brussels (detail), 1889. Ensor. Casino Communal, Knokke-le-Zoute, Belgium.

Head of a Prophet, 1912. Woodcut. Nolde. National Gallery of Art, Washington, D.C. (Rosenwald Collection).

Child Consecrated to Suffering, 1935. Gouache. Klee. Albright Art Gallery of Buffalo.

Death Tears a Child from its Mother (and) Death and the Child. Lithographs, 1935. Kollwitz. Collection Museum of Modern Art.

Christ and the Woman Taken in Adultery, 1917. Beckmann. Courtesy the late Curt Valentin, Buchholz Gallery.

The End of the World. Engraving by Posada. Collection Museum of Modern Art.

St. Francis and the Indian, 1923–24. Fresco by Orozco in the National Preparatory School. Photo courtesy MacKinley Helm and the Institute of Contemporary Art, Boston.

Migration, 1932–34. Fresco by Orozco in the Dartmouth College Library, Hanover, N.H. Photo courtesy MacKinley Helm and the Institute of Contemporary Art, Boston.

Detail of a fresco in the National Palace, Mexico City. Rivera.

Fisherman's Last Supper, 1940–41. Hartley. Collection Mr. & Mrs. Roy R. Neuberger, New York.

The Stoning of St. Stephen, 1943. Orozco. Collection Dr. Carillo Gil, Mexico City. Photo courtesy MacKinley Helm and the Institute of Contemporary Art, Boston.

Joy of Life, 1906. Matisse. The Barnes Foundation, Merion, Pa.

Icarus, 1947. Matisse. Cut-out paper illustrating the series *Jazz*. Courtesy Museum of Modern Art.

Les Demoiselles d'Avignon, 1907. Picasso. Collection Museum of Modern Art.

Crucifixion, 1930. Picasso. Owned by the Artist. Photo courtesy Museum of Modern Art.

Minotauromachy. Picasso. Etching, 1935. Collection Museum of Modern Art.

Guernica, 1937. Picasso. Owned by the Artist. On loan to the Museum of Modern Art.

Vence Chapel. Matisse. View showing altar, windows and figure of St. Dominic. Vence, 1951. Photograph by Helene Adant.

Vence Chapel. Matisse. View showing Stations of the Cross. Vence, 1951. Photograph by Helene Adant.

Suprematist Elements (pencil drawings), 1913. Malevich. Collection Museum of Modern Art.

Midi, 1954. Davis. Collection Wadsworth Atheneum, Hartford.

Garden in Sochi, 1941. Gorky. Collection Museum of Modern Art.

Number Eight, 1950. Pollock. Courtesy Sidney Janis Gallery.

Dark Over Light Earth, 1954. Rothko. Courtesy Sidney Janis Gallery.

Mathieu painting Battle of Bouvines. Photograph by R. Descharnes, Paris.

Art under Totalitarianism, I. The Art Magazine by Udo Wendel. Reproduced in Hellmut Lehmann-Haupt's *Art Under a Dictatorship*.

Art under Totalitarianism, II. Gavril Miklossy's "Grivitza, 1933."

Portrait of Joe Bousquet, 1947. Dubuffet. Collection the Author.

Mambo, 1954. Bigaud. Collection the Author.

The Thanksgiver, 1954. Matta. Courtesy Sidney Janis Gallery.

To Cover the Earth with a New Dew, 1954. Matta. Courtesy Sidney Janis Gallery.

Woman IV. De Kooning. Courtesy Sidney Janis Gallery, New York.

The Shore, 1953. Perlin. Courtesy Catherine Viviano Gallery and Dr. and Mrs. Cranston Holman, New York.

Cadaver II, 1954. Crayon. Bloom. Courtesy Durlacher Brothers.

Older Jew with Torah, 1945. Collection Mr. & Mrs. George W. W. Brewster, Brookline, Mass.

Drawing of a Man, Undated. Levine.

Battle's End, 1946. Levine. Collection Ruth Gikow.

Gangster Funeral, 1952–53. Levine. Collection Whitney Museum of American Art.

Barber Shop, 1946. Lawrence. Courtesy The Allan Gallery, New York.

American Family, 1954. Rosenthal. Bronze group for the façade of the Police Facilities Building, Los Angeles. Courtesy the Artist.

Christ on the Cross, 1948–51. Matisse. Artist's proof of the altar Crucifixion for the Chapel at Vence, France. Courtesy Museum of Modern Art.

Incubus, 1954. Shahn. Collection Mr. & Mrs. E. R. Bahan.

Index